WE
ANIMALS

Stories

EMMA BIDER

DeeBee

WE ANIMALS

Copyright © 2020 by Emma Bider.

For information contact :
emmabider@gmail.com
www.emmarbider.com

ISBN: 9781896794402

First Edition: December 2020

10 9 8 7 6 5 4 3 2 1

Acknowledgements

Many people deserve many thanks for contributing to this book. Thank you first and foremost to the Propeller Coffee Writing Club, who saw most of these stories before anyone else and who always offered helpful, thoughtful and honest feedback on all my weird writing ideas. Part of this book is for you. Thank you to my first readers, Pascale, Renée and Tyler, your comments shaped the final draft of this book, I couldn't have done it without you. Thank you to my muses (you know who you are) and my parents, who are avid readers and ensured I would become one too. Eric Murphy is the genius behind this book cover, thanks for creating something so beautiful. I hope people do judge my book by this cover. Thanks to David Hamilton, my wonderful publisher for helping me see this thing through to the end. Thanks most especially to Tyler Hale, my love, my biggest supporter, my champion. Thank you for reading all my work and for always setting me straight when I thought I couldn't or shouldn't be doing this.

Contents

If / Then

IF GODS DID NOT NEED TEMPLES THEN...IF THE EARTH HAD
not turned white then...If forests weren't so complicated
then...If fire never caused smoke then...If the world was flat
then...If sugar wasn't so delicious then...If coal didn't burn so
well then...If feathers weren't great accessories then...If we
thought dogs had souls then...If farmland didn't seem infinite
then...If we'd asked where the sewers ended then...If we'd
listened to the poets then...If collection wasn't a science
then...If more children survived infancy then...If we didn't
need to know everything then...If food were never a
bargaining chip then...If difference wasn't tyrannized then...If
foresight was 20/20 then...If progress was different from
excess then...If we'd moved beyond mere usefulness then...If
pesticides were never invented then...If nature never equaled
nation then...If we'd listened in 1827 then...If we'd listened

in 1937 then...If we'd listened in 1956 then...If we'd listened in 1990 then...If we ever shut up and listened then...If smog killed rich but not poor then...If clean water was not a commodity then...If pandas got off on being watched then...If money was not a virtue then...If we didn't need so much light then...If the state wasn't part of the problem then...If oil was never discovered then...If Ken Saro-Wiwa had lived then...If fish had better PR guys then...If ice had a higher melting point then...If we chose to lose money on purpose then...If it wasn't so political then...If we'd only realized then...

But we didn't, so here we are. We are here.

The Wolf Attack

THIS IS THE TRUE STORY OF ARTIUM KALICHAVA AND THE wolf. Not the story told by Yanich Okulov to all the village. No, this is the story of Artium, a recently widowed man, (though he still has his health and a fine head of hair), a man who rented land from the state in order to farm, a man who lived in a valley of the Caucasus mountains far away from anything very important.

Artium was, in general, happy with his lot (no, not in general, very happy really, with everything he had, he muttered to himself while tossing in bed). True, there were a few more military uniforms around the village into which Artium occasionally ventured than he would have liked, and sure there were a few more terrorists flitting their eyes this way and that in the alleyways of that same village than Artium was particularly comfortable with, but all in all, his was a good, modest life.

Artium got out of bed one morning after appraising his

situation in this manner, which he found himself doing quite often these days. He was greeted by a nasty November wind blowing snow under the door as he went to tend to his cows and bull (ah, no; the cows and bull of the state), and then tend to the nation's fine, not at all scrawny chickens.

The sun not yet risen, Artium could not see his beloved mountains. The ones where he grew up and hunted, the ones that sheltered him and his family in even less pleasant times than these. He paused regardless and looked on in their direction before making his way to the barn.

Not for the first time, Artium wished his son was still alive to help him with the daily chores. His back often ached when he tossed hay to the cows and the bull, and his fingers swelled in the cold when he tried to make minor repairs to the barn roof (he was lucky his home was made of stone and the roof was re-tiled before the bombings had begun anew).

Soon he would need to hire a farm hand or coerce a tired terrorist into taking a break from his righteous work and enjoy a straw bed and occasional meagre bowls of stew instead. This would provide Artium some company at least, for while he was grateful for his modest life, it was hard to be grateful all the time, and in rare moments (increasingly less rare moments) the darkness of eternal sleep seemed preferable to a long life alone.

Artium shook the thoughts out of his head again. He milked the nation's two cows and patted the bull on the forehead, noting the shine of his adolescent horns. It would soon be time for the slaughter.

Feeding the chickens, checking for eggs, Artium waited for the sun to rise before sending his livestock out to the sparse pasture across the dirt road. Already the morning had passed him by and still there was so much to be done (he felt only slightly obliged to thank God for the many days in his lifetime. He could always do the work for the nation tomorrow that he could not get to today).

Artium Kalichava's great gift was his affinity for remaining inoffensive. After his brother had been shot in the town square of Tbilisi, after his wife had been refused entry to the Stravropol hospital for looking too ethnic, after his child had been taken away in the dead of night, the powers that be remained indifferent to Artium. He did not believe this would last forever. He tried to be grateful for the extra time his great gift had given him (he would not be the well-fed wolf who nevertheless looked on towards the forest).

His wife dead, his son presumed dead, Artium wondered every day when death would return one more time for him. While he waited, he watched the mountains and the road, the cows and the weather for any changes. Any sign that such a day was upon him, that Fate had decided to look his way.

The following morning Artium had arranged for his neighbour, Yanich Okulev, to do the morning chores in exchange for milk. He woke earlier than usual and opened the heavy wooden chest that sat next to his bed. Inside was a rifle, his most precious item. It was an old model of the Putin era.

Out he went, rifle on his back, towards the mountains on wooden snowshoes in search of Roe deer or if he was very lucky, wild boar. Stalin, the Georgian prince, once claimed he'd killed a leopard in the valleys of Gori. Artium had never seen one and was unconvinced (though Stalin had been one of their great, ancient leaders indeed, for even when famine swept so many away there was always a scrap of bread or two at the ration counter, always some manner of paying if you could bear it).

Fading into the woods always calmed Artium's mind which usually flickered from thought to thought like candlelight. He did not get very far at all into the wintry depths of his beloved Caucasus firs when he was met with a wolf directly in his path.

Had the wolf been waiting for him? (Fate does play his games in all manner of ways). No, the wolf looked well-fed and brawny, ready to take on another brutal winter. And yet. Artium, eyes widening, dropped the rifle. This could be the death knell. This could be the trigger he was too cowardly to pull himself. So clear did the thought strike him, that Artium Kalichava swore he heard church bells from the village, ringing as they would for a funeral.

He made a decision. Artium carefully took off his snowshoes and sank in the snow, until only his torso was visible. The rifle's snowy indent was just visible beside him. Artium closed his eyes and resigned himself to Fate.

The wolf looked on, perhaps with curiosity more than malice, until his ears cocked southward, his muscles tensed, and his tail sprang to attention.

Artium did not see his soon to be slaughtered bull careening through the snow towards the wolf and the wolf, perhaps shocked by the sight, did not move. He lifted his head and howled. Artium heard the bull dragging its determined body through the snow, the wolf's snarling and barking. He felt the swift air behind his ear as the bull plowed past his sunken body. The wolf was running now, though in what direction Artium could not say. He could hear the disturbed snow. It dusted his face. The sound of growling approached and despite himself Artium tensed and cringed, when suddenly the growling was cut off, replaced with a desperate, alarming yelp. Artium opened his eyes to see the bull's young horns driven deep into the wolf's neck.

Blood spread out over the snow. The bull struggled to release his horns from bloody tendons and fur. The blood trailed down towards Artium's indentation in the snow, while he struggled to lift himself back onto his snowshoes to help the bull free.

Breathing hard, Yanich the neighbour paused in front of the scene, having chased the bull through the snow and trees.

"Artium. That bull ran out of the barn and did not stop. He must have known something…was happening," Yanich wheezed.

Yanich saw the wolf. Miraculously, it was still breathing. He grabbed Artium's rifle and shot the prostrate body. The wolf stilled.

"Better he not suffer," said Yanich.

"I will not slaughter this bull," Artium swore as he and his neighbour made their way out of the trees.

The bull was a messenger. It was not his time and he should go on living. They returned to the barn and Yanich took the milk he was owed and not another word was said between them.

Two months later the shelling had cut off food supplies and a series of terrible ice storms cracked Artium's barn roof. The bull died of frostbite on an unusually frigid January evening that left even Artium, in his fire-heated home, shivering and breathless. He harvested the bull's frozen body for meagre cuts of meat and brought the cows and chickens into the house. Yanich had been telling everyone in the village about the savage wolf attack, the hero bull, the miracles of chance and luck. Artium shivered next to the chickens, wondering why Fate spent so much time eradicating his every chance at eternal peace.

"Why not me?" Artium asked his companions as they huddled under a few scratchy blankets.

The animals did not have an answer.

Getaway

THREE WEEKS. FOR THREE WHOLE WEEKS SMOG BLANKETS the city. Kira's office transitioned to work from home last Friday and now it is Friday again and meteorologists are saying the smog could be getting worse. Kira works in the bedroom. Seth is trying to help an elderly woman sort out her will over the phone in the basement. The school closed today, sending Leo home with a strict note about how his education must be taken seriously while he's at home. Of course they invited Orit to stay with them. Her place is down in St. Henri and theirs is near the mountain.

Westmount, their neighbourhood, is for the rich and fancy as Orit never fails to mention. They would never have been able to afford a place here if it hadn't been for Kira's aunt, a beloved and exuberant Haitian woman Kira stayed with during her childhood summers. Kira's aunt won the lottery at sixty and secretly bought the house, leaving it to a shocked Kira when she died. They'd moved in a month ago.

The air is only moderately clearer here, but it is enough. Orit has asthma, she is seventy-four and, crucially, she is Kira's mother-in-law so she can't exactly say no.

Three weeks is an eternity. There is something exquisitely exhausting, Kira thinks, about nearing forty and trying to write emails on a milk and Honey Nut Cheerios-stained couch, while your husband starts calling the basement his bat cave. Every morning Kira wakes up at six, exactly ten minutes before her alarm, and gets in the shower before Leo comes in and takes command of her morning routine. Since having a child Kira can shower in under four minutes. Normally she sets the coffeemaker every night and reads the news while getting dressed. Leo appears exactly when the alarm goes off. That is their deal: when he hears the alarm he can come in, not before. Most of the time he follows this rule.

Kira has always been praised for her efficiency and pragmatism. They are qualities she mentions in job interviews. The smog derails her. It's May and she can't open any windows. There are no bird sounds to greet her in the morning and the sun is never out.

No one knows exactly how it started either. Seth reads everything he can find in between client meetings. Lately he's been moving into conspiracy theory territory. It's a government attack to lower the population. It's an industry leader holding the region hostage until a ransom is provided. The smog was deployed by China, the US, Russia. The most widely believed theory—the one journalists are reporting—is that a volcano erupted in Iceland, coinciding with a freak anticyclone over the city. There have been no reports out of Iceland about an eruption that Kira can find. Or anywhere in Europe, despite the climatologists online saying this is the only realistic cause of the current crisis. The city feels cut off from the rest of the world.

Yesterday she started reading about coping skills in a natural disaster. She reads articles telling her how to talk to Leo about global catastrophes and pivot the conversation into a "learning opportunity" about climate change. Leo doesn't want to learn. He sits at the kitchen table eating his cheerios and asks when he can watch TV. Orit sits next to him, picking at plain toast and wondering aloud if Kira has read that study connecting childhood behavioural problems with too much screen time. No. Kira has not.

Orit spends most of her days wandering through the house, commenting on its flaws.

"Did your aunt get the place inspected before she bought it? I swear I can feel a slight tilt to the floors. Probably a crack in the foundation."

"Kira, you are planning to redecorate right? Some of these colours are just too gaudy, don't you think?"

"I've just never been in such a house," she says. "The property taxes must be through the roof. You're sure you can afford it?"

"She's driving me crazy," Kira whispers to Seth at night. "You need to help me with this."

"I know. I'm sorry. It won't be much longer though. I mean, it can't be."

"But we don't know that!"

Kira is learning about emotional regulation through an app. She's probably doing it wrong. She often fails to keep her voice calm, especially after reading articles that predict the smog will be around for at least a month.

The worst part, the reason pragmatic, efficient Kira has all but disappeared is that she has no outlet for the stress of

Smoggeddon. All the self-care articles say she needs an outlet. A way to "de-stress". She's terrified she'll scream at Leo, making him cry, or she'll break a plate, or tell Orit to shut up. Another Friday comes. Week four. Something must be done.

"We need to have sex," says Kira.

It's late, Orit and Leo should be asleep.

"We can be quiet."

Seth puts down his phone.

"Yeah, sounds great," he smiles.

It's a relief to see he needs it too. How could he not? Just as things get going, they hear a knock at the door. Kira throws on an old shirt, goes to open the door.

"Yes sweetheart."

"I can't sleep," says Leo.

The next three nights Leo comes into their room and begs and cries to sleep in their bed. They are both too tired to argue for long.

New tactics are devised. Kira discovers the attic. Starts concocting a plan. After further inspection it's clear that while roomy, the attic is too dusty. She closes it back up. The garage is too conspicuous and there's a risk Leo will see them and think they're going grocery shopping or something. The laundry room is right next to Orit's room, who is a light sleeper. She always seems to pop out of nowhere when Seth and Kira are scheming. She asks about getting cable or driving back to her place to get more wool for her knitting.

"Do you think Leo would like to learn bridge? Or some other card game, they're never as good with only three."

It's all understandable, she's bored, but Kira wants to shake her. She wishes there was somewhere Orit could go without having to go out into the dangerous air. Kira refocuses on their mission. Smog-related news goes unread and she buys yarn and needles for Orit online to keep her quiet. She discovers a crawl space beneath the basement stairs. Is there a way to test how soundproof it is? She wonders if lining the walls with egg cartons really would muffle the noise.

"I HAVE A SURPRISE," SAYS SETH ONE AFTERNOON, WHILE Orit and Leo are both napping. He goes to a high cupboard in the kitchen.

"I ordered them online. Cost a fortune."

He pulls out two military-grade gas masks.

"We can go outside now."

"Your mom doesn't like it when we leave. You know she's not comfortable watching Leo alone."

"We can go at night."

Kira hesitates. She is imagining them on the ground, or up against a tree, unable to kiss, barely able to see, groping at each other in the thick air.

"I don't know."

"Can we just try it? Please?"

He didn't specify exactly how much they cost. Kira sighs. Seth leans in and kisses her.

"Let's just try."

She nods. Because the smog is still here, with no sign of leaving.

AT FOUR IN THE MORNING SETH'S ALARM GOES OFF. KIRA opens her eyes and immediately looks out the window. Still smog, only darker.

They throw on some clothes, Seth grabs a towel and

they don the masks before quickly stepping out into the dark. Kira feels a twinge of guilt as she locks the door. They won't be long, she thinks. Leo won't even notice.

She can't even see the other side of their street. Seth takes her hand and they slowly make their way along the sidewalk, towards the mountain. The grey, opaque air is less oppressive in the park. The trees seem to be keeping it at bay, though it might be her imagination.

Near the top of the mountain Seth takes his mask off. He takes a deep breath in.

"It's got to be over soon if we can breathe up here."

Kira just leans back against a tree, bewildered by what they are doing. It all seems so elaborate, so unnecessary now that they're here where the air is slightly clearer.

Then Seth lays the towel down on a discreet patch of new grass and pulls her into his arms. Kira feels that too-rare craving, that ache and warmth she's been missing. She lets go of her misgivings about their plan. It's a necessary, beautiful divergence from the complete breakdown she's been speeding towards ever since the smog descended.

After, Kira swears she sees a glimpse of the sun as she's putting her mask back on. They walk down through the park. When they turn onto their street, she looks up for it again, seeing nothing. The world has already returned to its grey and heavy state.

Transplant

IT HAPPENED ON A TUESDAY MORNING IN APRIL. MATTY and I were thirteen years old. The first thing I remember hearing over the radio was that all the schools were closed.

"Maybe something's happened at the mines," said Mom as she tugged on her coat to go to work.

"I'll call your father. See what's up. I guess you're coming with me today."

Halfway to the car she got a call and was told the university was shut down too. Matty pulled his phone out of his pocket and looked up the news. There they were. Nine volcanoes dripping in tropical foliage looming over Sudbury. We ran out to the driveway and could even see their soft smoke floating in the air.

There wasn't much information on the first day. Matty and I sat in the backyard, absently stepping in muddy puddles and discussing this new geographic anomaly.

"You think they just grew up all the sudden, like islands?" I asked.

Matty was watching a live stream of a farmer walking the dividing line between the northern Ontario birch and pine, and the tropical palms and man-sized ferns.

"No way. The ecology is all wrong. Besides we're not on a ridge line. If we were, there'd be volcanoes here already."

Matty had been obsessed with ecology since he was three years old and trying to eat bugs. I was always more interested in rocks. Once, apparently, we were found side by side in the backyard, passing rocks and bugs to each other, like a couple swapping food they didn't like from each other's dinner plates. A favourite story of our mother's.

We lived right on Elm street, our backyard facing the road, so we had a prime view of the traffic heading up to the mountains. The tanks came first, trundling up the road with slow purpose, their long cannons pointing north. Behind the tanks were armed personnel vehicles, then a couple of cars Mom thought were probably journalists, then the local TV crews, a couple of minivans driven by shaggy-haired scientists in Gore-Tex rain jackets and finally police, who were knocking on doors telling everyone to stay inside.

"What's going on?" Mom asked when the police came to our door.

"That's classified ma'am," said the officer. Just like in the movies.

Of course, Matty and I had our hypotheses. At thirteen we already considered ourselves adults, and, having attended what our father regularly called "that fucking hippie school", The Grove, for three years by then, we also felt qualified to provide our opinions on the unprecedented events going on.

"The plants have to be equatorial based on the foliage," said Matty, as I spied through the warped beams of our fence for anymore movement.

"Tim, didn't Ms. Meakin teach us a lesson on tropical ecology last month?"

"Maybe?" I said, watching four black SUVs race down Elm.

"Kids come inside, they're talking about it on the news!"

The reporter looked nervous. Soldiers were walking in and out of the frame. Mom had the volume on high, as Sudbury CBC tried to explain.

"We are in front of what appears to be the Virunga Mountain range, a string of nine volcanoes normally located on the borders of Rwanda, Uganda and the Democratic Republic of Congo."

"I knew it!" cried Matty.

"No you didn't," I said, punching him in the arm.

"Shhh," said Mom.

The reporter was about to continue when the camera was taken down and all we saw was the ground. We could hear the journalist trying to reason with who we assumed was one of the soldiers. Then the screen went black, before the station anchor abruptly returned to our screen, hand on her ear.

"We're…we're being told that as of right now, this is an issue of national security and…that journalists will not be allowed near the perimeter of the site. The mayor is being notified of the situation and the Prime Minister will provide a press statement this afternoon."

Then they went to the weather. Mom turned off the TV.

"How did this happen?" she said under her breath.

Matty was staring at the TV, his brow furrowed.

"Why won't they tell us what's going on?" he asked.

"Probably because they don't know themselves sweetheart." She turned to us. "Want to go for a drive?"

IT TOOK ABOUT TWENTY MINUTES BEFORE WE REALIZED Mom was taking a circuitous route to the university. Soldiers were posted at every major intersection, telling people to go home. At Regent and York, she told a younger looking guy that we were going to the hospital.

"Weekly blood transfusions," she said, and I even heard a gulp in her voice like she was about to cry.

Having never seen her like this before, Matty and I stayed quiet until we saw Laurentian's track ring and gym. There were no soldiers we could see. The place looked empty. When Mom finally parked by Science Building II, we were bursting with questions.

"Mom why are there so many soldiers around?"

"Why don't they let us see the volcanoes?"

"Mom, why are we at the university?"

She didn't answer. She just sighed and pulled out two granola bars from her purse. Like we were toddlers.

"Here," she said, "It's almost lunchtime. Now come on before someone sees us."

We'd been to the university many times before. After the divorce, Mom used to bring us in when she couldn't find a babysitter on PD days. We also got subsidized entry to the sports camps there, so every summer we spent two weeks running across campus, trying to escape our teenaged counselors to Lake Laurentian, just south of the gym. We knew the physics department too, where everyone referred to us as "Aisling's twins".

The physics department was on the fifth floor. We hiked up the stairs, Mom looking around, peering out of each floor's door before we reached the fifth. She leaned against the door and turned to us.

"Not a word."

Out the door and down the hall, we practically ran until we got to Mom's office, a cramped space with one wall covered by a whiteboard, and another piled with books that almost covered the only window.

"Sit," she commanded. We took off our backpacks and sat. Then she left for a few minutes before returning looking much more relaxed.

"Okay. Stay here please. You can play some games on my computer."

As soon as her footsteps were out of earshot, Matty got up and headed out the door.

"Where are you going?" I said.

"Bathroom," said Matty, smiling. I followed him.

He stopped in front of some double doors and crouched down, peering through the slight opening between them. Inside there was a large table, and ten people were sitting around it, some looking at their computer screens, others talking in little clusters. Mom was at the front of the room.

"Alright," she said, silencing everyone. "You know why we're here. Who did it?"

People muttered, no one saying anything louder than a whisper. I strained to hear a woman closer to the back say "here we go" under her breath.

"Why would it be one of us Aisling?" said a man near the front of the table.

He hadn't looked up from his computer.

"We all know no one here's even come close to even theorizing how this kind of teleportation might work."

"We don't even know whether teleportation is the accurate way to describe what's happened," said someone else.

"Look, guys, we've been working on quantum teleportation for decades now. We know more about particle transmission than any other physics department in the world. Who else would have remotely similar expertise in this field besides us?"

"Aliens?" said the woman sitting near the door.

She was slouched in her chair and scrolling through her phone. A series of nervous snickers rippled through the group.

"Yes, thank you Renée, very helpful."

"We can't rule out the possibility that a foreign power did this."

"I doubt it, Mitch."

"Besides, what would China gain from plopping a bunch of African volcanoes in Northern Ontario?" said someone we couldn't see.

"Whoever did this is an international security threat now. It had to have been someone we know. We need to figure out how they did this and who they are. Not only could this shut us down forever, it's also a breakthrough. We could be the first ones to successfully replicate large matter teleportation."

The room was quiet again, the scientists lost in thought. My legs were getting sore from crouching in front of the door. Matty was licking the inside of his granola bar wrapper, ignoring my gestures to be quiet.

"Explain to me again what the big deal is about having

these volcanoes magically appear in Sudbury?" said Mitch finally. "I mean, they've been in the news in the last couple of years, one of the last rainforest ecosystems on the planet, amazing mineral deposits, home of the last, what twenty mountain gorillas? Is it so bad they're here now? I bet there are fewer gorilla poachers in Sudbury."

"Jesus Mitch," said Renée rolling her eyes.

"Mitch the Rwandan President is already calling this an act of war. Someone stole their land. I know you're not a historian but surely you know how stupid you sound right now?"

"Hey, I'm not the one who brought a tropical ecosystem into a zone where it snows six months of the year."

"It had to have been someone old," said Renée suddenly, straightening up in her chair. "With access to the lab for decades."

"A professor emeritus or something?" said someone else, now typing something into her computer. "Someone who'd have access to the lab but who'd fly under the radar."

Mom nodded.

"I think you're right Olu. Okay here's what we're going to do. Renée, Olu and Angela I need you to do some lit searches on anyone who retired in the last couple of years. A particle physicist or one of our own quantum physicists. If they have access to the SNO lab, they definitely could be our person. Find out what they've published, if that can give us any clues, and do some deep dives here. See if there's anyone who's published in more radical alternative theory sites or journals."

"If he really managed to do this, it would have taken some pretty radical experimentation," mused Olu. "I mean, we've scaled up to molecular information transmission. If this is for real, then the process would have taken some serious energy outputs."

"We don't know if it's a he," Renée pointed out.

"Educated guess."

"Mitch, Raymond, Neha, I need you with me checking to see who's been looking at our molecular data. There's no way they figured this out on their own. The rest of you, I need you to see if there's been any weird activity, weather, or bursts of energy reported anywhere here or in either Uganda, Rwanda or the DRC. Olu's right, whoever did this must have had a transmitter or set off a moment of transmission that would have given off massive amounts of energy."

A busy silence took over the room. Mom and her team made their way to the door. We ran to the stairwell with just enough time to crouch down before they passed us.

"Can you believe it? The last gorillas in the world. Here," said Matty.

"I mean, seems to be like the least important thing."

"They should definitely stay right? I mean, how cool would that be."

"I don't know. It doesn't sound like they would survive."

"We have to go see them." Matty started going down the stairs.

"Wait! Why do we have to go see them? How would we even get there?"

"Tim," said Matty, whipping around. "When will you or I ever get to see the last great apes under normal circumstances?"

"I don't know—"

"Well I do. I've done the math. Plane tickets are only

getting more expensive. We don't have jobs and Mom can't afford to take us anywhere. We'd be waiting a minimum of what, five years before even thinking about flying to Rwanda? Orangutans are already extinct, chimps will be next. Those gorillas are normally so protected they barely even do tours to see them anymore and those cost like a million bucks."

Matty's voice was getting louder, his eyes wide. I'd never seen him this excited about anything before.

"You want to be a biologist though, why can't you wait until then?"

"They'll all be dead."

"You don't know that."

"I do."

"Jesus dude, that's a bit dramatic."

"I'm going Tim. Don't come if you don't want to. I'm going to see them." He continued down the stairs.

I could think of nothing else to do but follow.

We left Science Building II and headed towards the university's sky-rail station. The train went to the casino and to the Northern Ontario Observatory in Capreol, right at the edge of the mountain chain. Both spots were too obvious. Everyone trying to sneak past the army to see the mountains would be headed that way.

"Let's go to the airport. It's closed so no one's going to be there."

"How do you know it's closed?"

Matty flashed his phone at me.

"I just checked. Keep up."

"There's no way there won't be soldiers up there. The Prime Minister's supposed to be coming up."

"Not till tonight. Come on man lighten up," said

Matty, smiling now. "We're going to be the first people to see a Canadian gorilla!"

The airport was overwhelmed with soldiers. Matty told the one who stopped us we were heading to Wanapitei Lake.

"Is that allowed?" Matty said, his face a mask of annoyance and sarcasm.

The soldier rolled his eyes.

"Just get out of here."

We dashed out of the airport where there were still a few optimistic auto-Ubers waiting at the Arrivals gate.

"Dammit," said Matty. "We don't have a credit card."

"Well I guess that's the end of the road."

"We can just use Mom's account. You remember the password?"

"Yeah, but come on man she's going to murder us if she finds out."

"Like this is her biggest problem right now," said Matty.

We got in and typed mom's password onto the pay screen. The car drove up Old Mine Road and then over to Portelance.

"We should get out before Milnet," I said. A few tanks had passed us going south.

"Good call."

"Car stop," said Matty and the auto-Uber pulled over onto the dirt shoulder.

From the road we could see one of the peaks, now partially enveloped in mist.

"Oh my god," said Matty.

It was so surreal I started to feel dizzy. Matty grabbed my shoulder.

"This is the best thing that has ever happened," he yelled. "Can you believe this?"

Before I could respond I heard shouting far up the road.

"We have to go," I said.

Squinting, I could see a blockade up the road. Four soldiers were walking towards us.

"Come on!"

Matty crossed the road and jumped into the trees. I ran after him. I could hear one of the soldiers yelling in the distance.

"Hey! Stop!"

We pushed through the trees and underbrush until we came to a lake. Across from it we could see the rainforest. Huge ferns and vines were already pushing towards the lake, and there were stands of bamboo next to trees I'd never seen with thin trunks to match their long fan-like leaves. Everything was a vibrant green paired with dark wood. It looked especially bizarre across from our trees, still bare from winter, and the frost-covered ground we were trying to navigate. The lake, though not large, still presented a challenge.

"Should we go around?" I said.

"We don't know how far it goes. No way. We should cross it."

"Matty this is insane. We'll be soaking wet."

Matty took off his backpack and started taking his clothes off and stuffing them inside. He dipped his hand in the water and laughed.

"The water's warm!" He took off his shoes.

I stood there watching until he was down to his underwear. He didn't look at me, just stared straight ahead, and, right before he jumped in, he gave a loud, long yelp of joy.

"Wahoo!"

"Matty shut up!" He was already in the water.

I stripped and ran into the water too, scared I would lose him. I could hear rustling behind me now. I swam desperately, barely noticing that Matty was right, the water was bathtub warm.

I just made it to the other side when I heard voices. Matty was already half-dressed when he heard the noise too. Shirtless, he pushed through the huge ferns and into the forest. I dove to follow him, still in my underwear, and immediately my feet started stinging.

"Ow!"

"Shut up they'll hear you."

I could see even in the faint light of the forest that Matty's feet had red, circular welts on them. He turned right and stopped at a large tree trunk.

"We can get dressed here."

I leaned on the tree and tried to brush off the dirt from my feet before struggling with my pants.

"That was wild," said Matty, still panting. "You think they saw us?"

"I don't think so. I wasn't exactly looking behind me."

"Yeah, alright."

"My feet are killing me."

"Mine too."

Eventually we started walking again, wincing as our rashes rubbed against our socks.

"We should try to follow the elevation. Gorillas get pretty high up," said Matty.

"Seriously, Matty when did you get so obsessed with these gorillas? How could you possibly know where they are?"

"First, they're called mountain gorillas. So, you know,

they're high up. In the mountains. Second, I am not obsessed. I just know we have a chance to do something amazing, and you don't seem to get that. Third, do you even realize how many species have gone extinct since we've been alive that we'll never get to see? Do you even realize what it would mean to see one of the last twenty gorillas in the world?"

"See," I said, "When you talk like that, you sound obsessive."

Matty rolled his eyes. "That's because you don't care about nature"

"That's not true, I just don't think I need to see something to care about it."

"Well I think if you really care about something, then you take every chance you get to understand it and be with it and...know it."

"You sound like you're in love with them," I said, annoyed, but I couldn't muster any real anger. Matty sounded so serious, it scared me a little. I dropped the argument and we started walking.

We continued at a slow pace, navigating the muddy ground and trying to avoid what Matty eventually identified as stinging nettles. After about two hours of walking I checked my phone. The battery was almost dead. Six calls from mom, a dozen texts, and two notifications about the volcanoes.

"Matty, stop for a second," I said, looking at the latest news.

"What is it? Mom texting you?"

"It's not that. Check this out." I held up a news article up with pictures from the DRC.

"See that hole with the lava in it? That's apparently

where the Mikeno Volcano used to be."

"And now it's here, with nothing underneath it."

"Well I guess it has Sudbury underneath it."

"You know what I mean."

There were other pictures too, of farm fields cut in half, rock falls, and villages collapsing into the crater-like formations caused by the uprooting of the Virunga mountain chain. Next to these pictures were aerials of the volcanoes in Sudbury, ponds disappearing underneath tropical earth, reports of maybe six or seven houses crushed underneath. No word on how many people had been killed.

I pressed on a video of the latest joint press conference by the three African presidents.

"This is an unprecedented ecological disaster and the work of a terrorist," said the President of Uganda.

"Canada must find this monster who has torn our countries apart, stolen thousands of our citizens, and some of the most culturally and ecologically important land in the world."

"This is nuts," said Matty. "You really think whoever did this was a terrorist?"

"I don't know, I mean why would someone do it? It's kind of insane right?"

Matty just shrugged. I closed the app and we continued walking. A few minutes later we stumbled onto a narrow path.

"I think I hear someone," said Matty.

We jumped off the trail into a stand of dense trees and waited. Soon enough a group of soldiers walked past, accompanying twenty people who looked scared and totally confused. One guy, who looked only a little older than us in jeans and a red-striped t-shirt, had his phone out and was listening to a video loudly. It sounded like the same one we'd just watched.

"Come on."

After what felt like another few hours, just before the sun had set, the path widened, becoming hard dirt and then pavement. We arrived at a clearing that opened to a massive cliff face. A series of orb-shaped villas were terraced on the mountain side, and we had to crane our necks to see the highest ones, still glowing with the last bit of sunlight. The area looked abandoned. We could see some of the doors were open and could smell something cooking.

"This is perfect!" said Matty.

He started up a set of pebbled stairs that moved up the mountain. I followed him to one of the closest villas. The door was open. Matty used his phone to peer into the darkness. Eventually we found a battery-powered lamp.

"Look at this place."

"I guess it's for tourists."

"They must have food somewhere."

The villa had a kitchen and we began searching the cupboards until Matty found two chocolate bars. I opened the fridge and was greeted by beer, a few mangoes and what looked like a leftover's container.

"I bet there's a restaurant somewhere. We should go find it," said Matty, already eating one of the chocolate bars.

"I'm just going to eat whatever's here," I said.

The container had rice and beef in it, with a few fried plantains. I flopped on the couch and started eating. Next to me was a stuffed gorilla. There was a pacifier on the coffee table.

"This is freaky," I said.

Matty, ignoring me, sat down on the couch.

"You know," he said after a bit, "I once heard Mom and Dad having this huge fight because Dad wanted to take us on some trip around Europe like he did when he was a kid, and Mom wanted to save money for university, and said all the forest fires and riots made it too dangerous anyway."

"I never heard them talking about that."

"You were asleep or something. Anyway, Mom won, obviously. She kept on saying that it wasn't worth it, and we could travel on our own when we were old enough if we wanted to."

He paused, munching on the chocolate bar.

"It just made me realize, you know, we're stuck here."

"Stuck where? The whole entirety of North America?"

"You know what I mean! We're never going to have enough money to get anywhere really, really cool. Mom's a professor and she can't afford to take us farther than B.C. and we took the train that one time and it was the slowest thing ever."

"B.C. was pretty cool though."

"Yeah," Matty conceded. "I guess."

"I think we'll get places."

"You remember what we wanted to be when we were younger?" said Matty, tossing the candy wrapper onto the coffee table.

I was still picking away at the leftovers, as if eating them slower would absolve me of the guilt I felt eating them at all.

"Astronauts."

"Exactly. We were eight or something when China put a man on Mars. Now there's a bunch of rich people who are going to go live there when it gets too hot here."

I nodded, remembering the conversations Mom had with her friends over long dinners a few years ago. It all sounded like a fantasy to me.

"Isn't that a good thing?" I said, trying to recall some of their arguments. "I mean, we get Earth to ourselves, other people can go screw up another planet."

Matty just shook his head.

"We're going to be watching the world burn and everything is going to be total garbage. Sometimes I wish we'd never even been born."

It was dark despite the light from the lamp. I could barely see Matty's face, though I was pretty sure he was crying. It hurt to see my brother, usually so confident, so sure of every decision, sounding so incredibly hopeless. I remember thinking how young we were. An odd thought for a thirteen-year old, but it had been an odd day. I felt burdened by Matty's frustration with no idea what to do about it.

"The rainforest was pretty cool eh?" I said, feeling stupid as I said it.

"Tim," said Matty. "This is my only chance to ever see a gorilla. This is my only chance to ever be in a place like this."

He rolled onto his side and looked at me.

"You're going to come with me to find them tomorrow right?"

"Yeah man, of course."

"Good," he said. Then he wriggled over to the far end of the couch and lay his head on the couch pillow, kicking me to the other side with his feet, like nothing happened.

I WOKE UP TO THE SOUND OF SHRIEKING BIRDS. THE SUN was shimmering through the window, a warm burst of light as it poured through the clearing below. Matty was still asleep. I went to the bathroom, which had a fancy composting toilet, two toothbrushes and a comb that still had some hairs in it.

When I came back to the living room Matty was awake and rummaging through the fridge.

"Anything for breakfast you think?"

"Mangoes?"

By the time we finished struggling with the four mangoes we'd grabbed from the fridge the sun was lighting up the whole villa. I tried to check the time on my phone, but it was dead.

"We should get going," I said, with some vague idea that one only sees gorillas in the early morning.

We set off, cautiously at first, quickly confirming there was no one else around. We took the path back the way we'd come and took a left where the path split and snaked upwards into some mist. The thick underbrush eventually thinned out into a bamboo forest that Matty pointed out, with visible excitement.

"Gorillas eat bamboo. I was reading about it last night. We're definitely close."

"Like pandas?"

"Shh!"

A few minutes later the trail stopped in front of an open plain of flattened grass and ferns. We crouched down, waiting for something to appear. Matty's eyes were glued to the scene in front of us. It seemed to me like he was barely blinking.

I don't remember how long we waited, but I do remember desperately needing to pee when we saw him. Matty smacked my arm and pointed at movement in the trees on the other side of the clearing.

"Look!"

The gorilla was bigger than I was expecting, with an enormous head and huge, muscular arms. He was alone, and padded towards the center of the clearing, before sitting down and pulling at a bamboo stem. He started crunching it in slow, thoughtful bites. He didn't seem to notice us at all. It felt strange, a bit like spying on someone and I got the same feeling I had when we went into the villa the previous night. We shouldn't be here, I thought.

Matty was transfixed though, watching the gorilla with rapt attention and muttering something to himself that I couldn't hear. I couldn't wait any longer. I got on my hands and knees, crawled back down the path and then found a tree to pee on. Just as I was finishing up, I heard voices coming towards us. I ran over to Matty, forgetting to crouch down and I saw the gorilla turn to look at us

"Oh no."

"What are you doing?" said Matty, whisper-shouting and tugging at my leg to get down.

The gorilla made no effort to move, just looked at us and continued to chew. Matty looked confused for a second and I saw the excitement in his eyes fade, as if the gorilla's indifference made the experience less meaningful. Then I heard rustling behind us.

"Someone's coming."

"Do you see who?" said Matty, unmoving.

"Does it matter? Matty we have to leave."

"A few more minutes. I want to see if he'll do anything."

"Matty let's go—"

"Freeze! Hands in the air!" I dropped to my knees, my hands raised, my head bowed, terrified and relieved at the same time. I opened my eyes and saw Matty sprinting through the tall grass and bamboo towards the opening in the trees where the gorilla had come from.

"Matty!" I cried, my mind bursting with fear as I watched my brother run, thinking there was no way he's going to make it, they're definitely going to kill him.

The soldiers ran past me and stopped in the same place we had just been, no eyes for the gorilla, who, though now more alert, was still eating his bamboo stem.

"Kid! Stop!" said the soldier. The other one was taking aim.

"No!" screamed Matty, without pause, still running.

The soldier knelt down and I heard a click.

"Matty stop!" I wailed as the gun shot rang out.

Then everything went black.

I'D NEVER BEEN IN A HOSPITAL BEFORE. WHEN I WOKE UP, all I could think was that the room looked kind of dingy. Mom was sitting beside the bed. She gasped when I woke up and kissed me on the forehead.

"Oh my god Tim you're okay," she said lifting me up and hugging me.

"Where's Matty?" I said, panic rising in my chest.

He's dead, I thought. He must be dead.

"Matty's okay too. He's with your dad right now. He wanted to be here when you woke up, but we figured it would be better for him to rest up."

"What did they do to him?" I said. I started crying.

"Oh, honey it's okay. I know it must have been scary. One of the soldiers shot him with a rubber bullet in the arm. He's got a fractured elbow. The doctor said it would be okay in a few months. They told me what you were doing," she said, frowning now.

"What the hell were you guys thinking? Do you know how worried I was?"

"I'm sorry Mom, Matty just, he just really wanted to do it and I didn't want him to be alone but…"

I thought then of my mom going into her office, not finding us there, how upset she must have been, and I started crying harder.

Mom pulled me to her again and I hugged her hard.

"I'm really sorry," I said.

"I know my love, I know." She sat back.

"I think we know who did it," she said after a while.

"Really?"

"Yeah. We found out someone had been sneaking into the lab at night to do his own research. I don't know how no one noticed before. I guess he had the credentials."

"So, it was a professor?"

"Yup. One of our own. Ed Meevish. Retired for about ten years. We called the police, but when they got to his house…"

"What?"

"When they got there, he was dead. He'd shot himself. I think when he realized what had gone wrong, or what a huge problem he'd started, I think, well, I don't know. There was no note." She said. "We still don't know how he did it either."

"What happened to the gorilla?" I asked.

"What gorilla?"

"We were watching one when the soldiers found us."

"So you saw one eh? What was it like?"

"It was like he didn't care that we were there at all." Mom laughed.

"I guess he had more important things to worry about."

I shrugged, still not sure how I felt about it. Then a nurse came in and told us I was allowed to go home.

THERE WASN'T MUCH TIME TO TALK TO MATTY ABOUT the whole thing in the days after we got back from the hospital. Mom had invited a Congolese family to stay with us while they waited for flights back home. The room we normally shared now included two additional brothers, so there was no opportunity for privacy. In any case, Matty spent most of his time pestering them with questions about their lives and was soon practicing Swahili at breakfast.

Various scientists from a range of fields had concluded decisively that there was no way the Virunga Mountain range's delicate ecology could survive a Canadian winter, even one decimated by climate change. The decision had been made to engage in a global effort to repatriate as much of the area's wildlife back to the Congo Basin region as possible, which, if nothing else, meant that tensions with the three African nations involved were cooling down, though were still a concern. The fate of the gorillas, who'd now lost a significant portion of their habitat back home, was still being determined.

The ecology and geology departments at Laurentian were at the forefront of the conservation effort thanks to their proximity to the mountains. They hired hundreds of research assistants and volunteers to help identify as much of the flora and fauna of the mountains and obtain cuttings and samples for conservation. Mom knew some people on the teams and managed to get Matty and I volunteer spots. When he wasn't at school or practicing Swahili, he was back in the mountains, learning to identify various ground insects and butterflies. I was studying the soil and rock formations, learning how much of the geological integrity of the volcanoes could be maintained. I barely saw Matty all summer.

Millions of dollars were poured into solutions, while Mom and her department continued to try and uncover how Ed Meevish had transplanted the mountains. When winter came, as predicted, the plant life immediately froze and died off, though the alpine regions of the volcanoes held up a bit better.

MATTY IS A WILDLIFE BIOLOGIST NOW, NO SURPRISE, AND travels between and the Congo Basin and Canada all the time, though it costs him a fortune. I am still finishing up my PhD in geophysics, studying the effects of the transplant on both the host land and the mountains themselves. We drifted apart after that summer, never really returning to a sense of closeness. We went to different universities and now speak to each other maybe once a month.

I've thought a lot about how our little adventure might have changed us. Certainly, it influenced our future careers and how we understood the world. Yet when I think back on that specific moment, when we saw the gorilla, what I felt was more akin to embarrassment than anything else. At that moment I realized that I had only a surface-level understanding of our own planet. In fact, I knew so little about the gorilla in front of me, it was almost like watching an alien go about his business in a universe wholly unfamiliar. It was this feeling I wanted to discuss with Matty in the days and weeks afterwards. On the rare occasions I tried, he dismissed me, or changed the subject. I believe now he felt exactly as I did and still refuses to accept what we both know is true.

I was embarrassed because up to the moment we saw him, despite my reservations, part of me believed I deserved to be there, watching this gorilla traipsing through the mountains that had dropped into our lives. I was ashamed. Matty, on the other hand, with his eyes glued to the creature in front of us, was trying to get the gorilla to see that he was different somehow, if only he could look the gorilla in the eyes and explain. He was worthy of being there when no one else was.

Tiger Baby

ALI PARK LOVES VANCOUVER INSTANTLY. THE PARKS, THE sushi, the well-toned runners and cyclists that pass her on their way to work, it all feels right. On clear days you can see the mountains from her tiny apartment in Richmond. It's early May and everything is already in full bloom. She loves the cheerful women she volunteers with at Waterways ("Guardians of oceans, lakes and rivers"). On her birthday, just a month after she arrived, the volunteer coordinator gave her a Waterways water bottle. It was so sweet.

This is why she had come, really. The sense of optimism and everyone's do-good attitude was unlike anything she'd experienced before.

Her friends back home don't understand why she's here though they're jealous of the warmer weather. Her mom calls her often and worries about how Ali will pay rent. Everything is expensive in the birthplace of Greenpeace, the corporate home of David Suzuki Foundation, Ecojustice,

Earthsave, Canadian Parks and Wilderness Society, and so many others. Ali has always wanted to work in conservation. It doesn't matter that her mom remains unconvinced, or that her friends don't like her Instagram photos anymore.

She knows she could have gotten an environmental job in Toronto. Except it's not only about a job. Upon moving, she started buying more organic vegetables. She'd made a pact to only buy locally made or used clothing and so far, she's stuck to it. She's taking shorter showers. It really does feel like she is changing into the Vancouver version of herself.

Today is Ali's first Human Extinction meeting. She walks into in a warehouse-style cafe, with exposed ceilings and metal-framed chairs. There are maybe fourteen people sitting around a few long wooden tables. She has never been to this kind of meeting before. A barista at Fresh Press, the coffee shop Ali sits in while sending out resumés, had told her about it.

"It's not as radical as people think," said Eve, when Ali remarked on a Human Extinction flyer at her table.

"I like to think of it as choosing to save the Earth instead of saving, you know, just the human species. It's a really selfless idea when you think about it. I don't need to procreate. But we're not like, suggesting that no one can."

Ali has not thought much about kids but agrees with Eve. It's not like she needs them, not when the planet is on the verge of ecological collapse.

Ali sees Eve sitting at the edge of the group. She joins her just as a tall woman wearing plum lipstick and a faded black tank top gets up and addresses the group.

"Welcome everyone, nice to see so many new faces. My name is Harper."

They go through the agenda. Mostly they talk about the

movement's lack of media coverage. More people were attending meetings around the world, yet their impact was reserved for slow news days or mommy blogs calling them eco-fascists.

"We need a hook," says Harper, "and we need a better way of distancing ourselves from that rhetoric. Our mission is as much about combating consumerism as it is questioning why we should bring more people into the world, just so they can suffer in the climate crisis."

Harper is articulate and ready for any argument. She knows the difference between compassionate anti-natalists and misanthropic ones. She can argue for or against both and sound convincing. Ali thinks she'd be a great mentor. She's dedicated. Driven. Harper works in conservation for a biotech company, just like Ali wants to.

After the meeting, Eve introduces Ali to Harper. It feels good to know them both. The whole group is invited to a new bar Eve knows. A cute place that specializes in modern tiki drinks. It is the highlight of Ali's limited, increasingly budget-conscious social calendar.

AT FIRST, ALI'S DAYS SPED BY. SIX MONTHS INTO THE JOB hunt, they have slowed to an aching shuffle. Still no job in sight, despite her many volunteering gigs and countless resumé iterations.

Every day Ali wakes up at six-thirty, showers, puts on a nice top and dark jeans and goes to Fresh Press to send out job applications. She is part of a cohort of regulars. She fantasizes about each of their lives whenever she feels her momentum flagging. There are always jobs to apply for, but she is rarely offered an interview. While she laughed off her new HE friends' concerns about her first Vancouver Fall, she is disappointed now to recognize her own low mood is a symptom of the endless gray weather and dark mornings. When the sun does appear, Ali sometimes feels compelled to get on her knees in gratitude.

Ali's mom calls and offers her money. She doubles her shifts at Waterways in the hopes of applying for a paid gig there. Nothing opens up. Writing op-eds and doing park cleanups are not leading to any useful connections either. Ali wants to ask her fellow volunteers what they do, yet every time she tries, she's too aware of her own desperation. She can hear the conversations in her head. They make her cringe.

One guy Paul, who wears Patagonia fleeces to do cleanups, once told her he worked at a bank.

"Oh really? Like what kind of stuff?"

"Just boring stuff. You don't want to hear about it."

She didn't ask him about it again.

She sees Eve and Harper more and regales them with tales of the job hunt. There was the woman who stared at her for five minutes before saying anything during an interview. There was the ad for a "tasteful stripper", which turned out to be a salaried position with a marketing agency. Eve asks her manager if there's an opening for Ali at the café. It's easier to stay hopeful when they're around. She can laugh with them about it all.

IN DECEMBER ALI STARTS WEARING AN OLD HOODIE TO Fresh Press and avoids looking at anyone. She is determined now to apply for every retail job she can find. She has started the terrible habit of ticking off every day on her calendar that she still doesn't have a job. She has dreams where she is at home, her mom quietly sipping coffee in the kitchen. It's such a relief that Ali wants to cry. But slowly, painfully, the dream falls away and she is still in Vancouver, alone. A beautiful place with nothing for her, where she does not belong.

She continues to attend HE meetings. The group is studying passages of David Benatar's book *Better Never to Have Been*. Ali has never heard of it.

"Does anyone else think it's interesting he's from South Africa? He lived through Apartheid. That clearly shaped his views," says Eve at one point.

Eve studied human rights. Ali wishes she could come up with something intelligent to say about the book. She's embarrassed to admit she hasn't read much on the philosophy behind the movement. The book gives her a headache. She would rather focus on what they can do to make things better than on all the reasons not to be alive. Maybe the author thinks it's all too far gone. She doesn't join in on the heated debate.

After the meeting, Harper invites Ali to join them at a pop-up bar that only sells super expensive wine and pairs it with gourmet hot dogs. The place is in a dark basement in Yaletown. The poor lighting gives Eve and Harper an orangey tinge as they scoot into a booth near the back wall. They look at Ali with sincere concern and order a round.

"Look, Ali, we know things have been hard. It really does take everyone like a year to two to figure it out here."

"Seriously," says Harper. "I'm from here and it's not easy to figure out. Trust me though, you're going to get through this and find something."

Ali is stunned they even knew she was struggling. Did she complain too much? Or was it awkward instead of funny to listen to her stories about the time that manager was high, or when she got forgotten in the lobby for an hour?

"I'm sure you're right" she says, trying to sound reassured.

"It feels hard to stay motivated is all."

They talk about other things for a while. Somehow, Ali has bought a second glass of twenty-six-dollar wine. She drinks it too fast.

"I'm so scared I'm going to waste my life, you know?" she says, interrupting Harper's story about new farm to table restaurants in town.

Ali notices a quote on the back wall "Wine comes in at the mouth, and love comes in at the eye". Stupid. Meaningless. Like this whole city. It makes Ali think of someone pouring wine in their eye. It makes her want to puke.

"Ali, it's going to be okay," says Harper.

Now their nodding reassurances are making Ali cry. She has tried for so long not to cry over her situation, which isn't even so bad, compared to other people. Now she's bawling in a public place, humiliating herself.

"Why don't we all go over to my place tonight and we can just talk and eat ice cream, and watch a bad movie," says Eve.

They're outside now. Harper and Eve are holding Ali between them, stumbling to the bust stop. She feels the weight of her plans and whatever other vague aspirations she had for coming here and being someone, doing something.

"Ali," says Eve, waking her up.

"Listen. You're going to do something amazing. You're smart and hardworking. You care about the world. You're having a bad night, you'll get through it!"

They do go to Eve's place. Ali makes it to the apartment

without throwing up and passes out in Eve's tidy bed. When she wakes up, the night is a blur, though she cringes at the memory of crying in the bar. The others are already in the kitchen eating breakfast. Eve makes her some herbal tea. Harper passes her a business card across the table.

"Remember how I said HE needed like, a hook to get people finally caring about our mission? I think this is it. One of our chapters in the States told me about it. Eve and I have talked about it and we're going to do it. We think you should do it with us."

Ali hugs Harper hard. Harper describes the company, what they do, the rules, the possibilities. Ali feels better than she has in weeks. Later at home she looks up company's website. It's called NewFruit. There's a slogan splashed over the top of the page: "Green Surrogacy for a Plentiful Future".

A MONTH AFTER FILLING OUT THE NECESSARY PAPERWORK, Ali is standing in front of NewFruit's office in the west end. She is waiting for Harper and Eve and feels conspicuous in her jeans and no-name jacket as she walks by all the glistening high-rises.

When they finally arrive, Ali feels a sense of warm anticipation, a feeling she now associates with their friendship. They enter a red brick building and are greeted by an immaculate waiting room with a white couch, soft-edged chairs and beech wood floors. A huge bay window floods the room with light. Across from the window is a large wooden desk that hems in a petite blonde woman Ali might have described as light or bright, or other words that describe someone sincerely optimistic about the world.

"Wow," whispers Eve.

"Welcome ladies!" says the woman behind the desk.

"I'm Lily. It's so nice to meet you all in person!"

Lily's hair is pulled back in a flawless ponytail. She rises from her chair, revealing a white silk dress. Ali wonders how she sits without ever creasing the fabric. Lily gestures at them to sit in the lobby, so they huddle onto the couch.

"I'm just printing out some final paperwork before the medical assessment, but don't worry I'm pleased to say you're all excellent candidates."

"In the meantime," she says, passing them pink iPads, "we'd love to get your feedback on something we're trying out for promotional purposes! We've been giving it to other clinical trial members and there's been a really positive response!"

Ali smiles at Lily and opens the only app on the iPad. It's a quiz. "What animal are you most compatible with?"

"Oh my god," says Harper. "Are you serious?" Lily beams.

"Yep! We want the process to feel as accessible as possible. In our ideal world, women will see their choice of animal for surrogacy as integral to their identity. We want them to think of this as an investment in their personal brand!"

Ali thinks it's cute, if not a bit creepy. Harper gives them both a "can you believe this" look but she still takes the iPad. The quiz questions range from lifestyle choices (are you tidy or messy? Do you eat meat?) to personality quirks (do you sing in the shower? Would you call yourself a social creature?).

By the end, they're getting into it. Ali submits her answers.

"What'd you get?" Eve asks Ali. "I got aardvark".

"I got panda bear," says Harper with a small smile.

"I guess because I like to sit at home and eat bamboo shoots all day."

They laugh. Lily is coming towards them with a huge stack of papers.

"I got tiger," says Ali.

"That's great! I think that is a perfect fit," chimes in Lily.

Before Ali can ask what she means, Lily deposits some paperwork in front of them, including a contract for their monthly stipends. Twenty-five hundred dollars a month for being surrogates in NewFruit's clinical trials.

They take a picture together. Then Lily introduces the doctors who will inseminate them. They explain the birth process, and where the animals will be sent when they are born. They are shown pictures of various animal sanctuaries, and a short video about NewFruit's relationships with "local knowledge holders" around the world.

Then they explain, in careful, mechanical language what the potential risks are. Infertility; thyroid complications; high blood pressure; very unlikely though still statistically possible auto-immune disorders. Ali stops listening at that point. She looks at the others. She thinks they look scared, which makes her feel better for feeling a bit freaked out. They are taken to separate rooms. "Good luck!" they say to each other as the doors close behind them.

The medical assessment takes at least an hour. The insemination on the other hand is brief and painful. Ali is told she has been implanted with four tiger embryos, that she may experience light bleeding and that she has to start taking her hormonal suppositories as soon as she gets home.

She is the first one back in the lobby. Lily is once again

sitting behind her desk. It's amazing, Ali thinks, how well she matches the office décor.

"How did it go?"

"It was fine. A little awkward."

Lily nods. "That is completely understandable. And I would take tomorrow off work too if you can. The hormonal changes are going to hit pretty hard."

"Right…Shouldn't be a problem. I don't actually have a job right now unfortunately."

Ali can feel herself turning red again, wishing the others would hurry up so they can leave.

"Oh my gosh," Lily shakes her perfect ponytail. "Finding work here is the worst! What's your field?"

"I'm looking for work in biotech," says Ali, then without thinking blurts out "I've done work on embryos actually. In school."

It's almost true. She took one class in genetic engineering.

"That's so interesting! You know," Lily leans closer to Ali, "We have a job coming up in our marketing department and they're looking for someone with a science background. You should apply!"

Before Ali can say anything, Harper and Eve are in the lobby and Lily has turned her attention to them. Eve decided to go with polar bears, instead of aardvarks. Harper got her pandas, and Ali stuck with tigers.

I HAVE ANIMALS INSIDE ME, ALI THINKS. SHE FINDS SHE needs to remind herself sometimes, because it's still hard to believe. Though the weekly visits to NewFruit's team of doctors, the strict diet and the initial puking all help make it feel very real.

She has a long list of medications she has to take, a detailed catalogue of photos NewFruit''s marketing department wants and endless medical appointments she has to get to. The first time she saw an ultrasound of the four tiger fetuses, they looked like tiny shrimp. The doctors assure her they will grow faster than she knows. They are right. When she is able to see their little paws and ears, Ali begins to have nightmares of the tigers clawing at her stomach until they tumble out of her maimed body. She starts to eat more red meat than probably necessary. She reminds herself that they are doing something amazing. Something that could support conservation efforts around the world, though Ali does sometimes feel like an object. A vessel for doctors to poke at. When she feels this way, she tries to remember that even if that is the case, even if she's merely a repository for embryos, at least she is not carrying more humans. Her body is carrying a different kind of future.

At their HE meetings, everyone asks lots of questions. Harper answers them mostly, with Eve and Ali chiming in once in a while. Yes, they take hormone suppositories, but actually the hormonal cocktail that appears in pregnant mammals is not so different from our own. Yes, insemination is super awkward, like the worst pap smear you've ever had with more bleeding. Gestation takes about three months. Once their pregnancies (and others going on around the world) are successful, NewFruit will start a global campaign to make human–animal surrogacy a real option for women.

"We're doing this to offer women a fulfilling alternative to bringing a human into the world. Once it's been approved, I think this will have to be our next campaign guys. It's a truly fulfilling experience."

Harper is glowing. The three of them are pioneers,

saving animals with their bodies. Saving the planet.

The first four weeks, the girls conclude, are brutal. They are all exhausted and poor Eve has especially terrible morning sickness. She has to take time off work. Ali gets up in the middle of the night to cry for hours. Harper says she is fine. Eve whispers to Ali one afternoon over lunch that Harper, in fact, has been an irritable bitch for weeks.

They are all reminded by the doctors that these experiences are normal. Yet Ali can't help but wonder, what is normal in a human/animal pregnancy? The sonograms are on her bedside table and she looks at them often. She tries to keep a diary of all the changes, the feelings, as she reasons it might be good for information packages for prospective surrogates. The world has taken on a dizzying new rhythm and Ali finds it almost impossible to keep up.

She spends hours staring at her computer. Tells herself she is looking for job ads while she scrolls through social media. She watches the NewFruit website for the promised marketing job, and when it appears, six weeks into her pregnancy, Ali applies. She gets an interview and she is offered the job a week later. Who else is more qualified to market animal surrogacy than one of NewFruit's own surrogates?

NINE WEEKS INTO THEIR PREGNANCIES, HARPER ASKS ALI and Eve to come over. Ali's been a little distant lately and it's hard to admit why. A few days ago while in the bathroom, Ali swears she saw the outline of a paw pushing out at her stomach. The experience left an ache in the pit of her stomach, knowing they'd be out of her so soon, alone in the world. She has to stop from speaking to them, naming them. Her new job is good, the people are great and supportive, but she can't tell them she's been scrolling through pictures of baby clothes and collecting other animal ultrasound pictures on Pinterest. To some extent this is due to all the marketing material she's been writing lately. Ali takes shots of her barely bigger stomach, part of a plan to reassure women who might be worried about weight gain that they won't have to buy new clothes when they become surrogates. She writes sentimental copy about the sanctuaries where their babies will end up and though writing has never been her strong suit, it feels like she could write forever about these paradises. She wonders if they'll ever get to visit.

When she gets to Harper's apartment after work, the girls are already waiting for her, sitting at a table in Harper's living room. Harper is sitting at one end, Eve on the other. Both are staring at their laptops.

"What's up?" Ali asks, taking a seat.

"How are you Ali?" asks Eve. "I feel like we haven't seen you in weeks."

"I know I'm sorry. I've been kind of busy lately. Nesting and stuff." She wishes it sounded more like a joke. Harper looks up.

"Good one."

Eve's lips are pursed. Harper looks back at her laptop screen.

"We need to talk to you about something."

She turns her screen to Ali. It is already dark outside and the screen glows like a hot flare.

"I got an email yesterday from am HE member in the States who's also doing the surrogate trial. Apparently NewFruit has preliminary results from other human trials they did in Vietnam."

"Okay. Is that a problem?"

"It's not a problem, except they told me that this year was the first round of human trials. The Vietnam ones happened two years ago. I don't know how Sandy got this information, but she says it's true."

"Basically, those first trials in Vietnam failed," says Eve.

"Most of the animals died, and so did some of the women."

"How…How could you not know about this?"

Ali feels her throat tightening.

"I thought you said they were legit."

"There's another thing," says Harper. She doesn't look at Ali.

"They showed us all those designated sanctuaries where the animals would be prepared for the wild. But after the email yesterday I started doing some more research."

Harper is tense, she looks like she's holding back tears. Eve turns on a lamp in the corner. Its yellow light gives the room a fuzziness that makes Ali feel tired and the room seem claustrophobic. Eve and Harper will still not look at her.

"We can't find any wildlife sanctuary affiliated with NewFruit."

"I mean, there must be a lot of them around—"

"We looked," says Eve.

"We both took the day off and looked. They never gave us any names because there aren't any."

"Why didn't you tell me when you called?"

"I'm going to go make some tea," Eve says instead of answering.

Ali pulls at the new grey cardigan she bought this week. A gift to herself. For how hard she's worked the last month despite the pregnancy. She can feel tears forming in her eyes.

"You seem quite attached to your embryos Ali," says

Harper. "We were worried about you. We wanted to make sure we had it right before we told you."

"It doesn't bother you?"

Now Harper looks at her for a long time and then she starts to sob, head in her hands, pushes her laptop away, collapses on the table.

"I'm so sorry I brought you guys into this" she says, and Ali gets up as Eve comes back from the kitchen.

They lean over Harper, hold her and cry together. They talk for a long time after about what to do, but for Ali it is hard not to feel like she is losing everything she's worked for this past year. They agree to follow through with the births, then expose NewFruit after, so at least they can be free of the animals inside them.

SOMEHOW, IT'S MAY AGAIN. ALI'S BEEN IN VANCOUVER A year. Her C-section is on Friday, just like Eve and Harper. Her boss gives her the week off, so she does a bit of shopping, trying and failing not to linger at baby stores or pet stores and trying not to cry when she spots the puppies in the window. She's been applying to other jobs. Once again, opportunities in her field are slim. They'll ask about the NewFruit job. It won't look good to have left only two months in. Maybe she will be able to explain why in a way that doesn't sound crazy. Ali thinks about this often when preparing cover letters on the sly at the office.

She still volunteers at Waterways. When she should be calling donors, she imagines going to a tiger sanctuary in India, knowing her little cubs, and them recognizing her as their womb mother. If they ever get there, that is, which she still wants to believe is possible. She's tried to gently probe Lily and her doctors, and one of them provides her with a brochure listing specific sanctuaries the animals are sent to. She's been too afraid to look them up. Instead she looks for volunteering stints overseas. She no longer goes to Human Extinction meetings, because going feels wrong. She's lied to all these people. The whole thing is a cascade of betrayal.

On Thursday Harper, Eve and Ali are eating lunch together on a quiet patio near the harbour. She is just finishing her salad when it happens. A clenching in her stomach. Ali hurries inside to the bathroom, pulls up her skirt and sees blood running down her thighs. She runs back out and Eve stands up, seeing the distress in Ali's face.

"Something's wrong," says Ali, in a loud, frantic moan, leaving any sense of calm behind.

She looks down. The blood has reached her calves. Eve and Harper half-carry Ali down the street.

"It's not that far, we're almost there," they say over and over again.

Ali is breathing heavy and thinking of the babies, the babies have to be okay, she can't let them die, and how the girls, they can't be carrying her like this in their conditions. She thinks about her collection of pictures, how they're more lies she's been telling herself and Ali starts sobbing, heaving big spastic gulps of air.

Then they get to the office, and Ali sees Lily look over at them in the doorway with alarm. Suddenly Eve and Harper are gone, and Ali is being pulled by the doctors to the birth room. She can hear herself screaming. The sound seems so far away.

THE CEILING IS BLUE. ALI FEELS LIKE SHE'S FLOATING IN warm water. It must be done, she thinks, but when she tries to get up, she realizes she can't feel her legs. She wants to hold her belly. Looking down at her stomach, she sees a slight, horizontal cut. It's a black hole, a portal to the best part of herself. And there's a person. Or actually, a tiger, standing near her feet. She tries to reach out to it, because it must be her tiger. It comes closer to her, like it's about to hug her, its face blank and untextured by fur or whiskers. Instead it moves towards the cut. Its paws that look like hands gently push apart the cut's edges. Another tiger appears on her other side and it's watching the first, holding a towel. They can't be mine, thinks Ali. The last thing she sees before the world collapses in on her is the hands as they reach inside her, searching for her babies.

Venusian

Log Entry 5,850: Thinking of Gloria, my Martian
May 9, 2089 (Earth Days, Earth Years)

I'VE BEEN THINKING ABOUT MARS LATELY. I HAVE A FEW theories as to why earthlings remain obsessed with it. Yes, it was the first planet officially colonized and yes, the atmosphere thickening experiments have so far been promising, but personally I think they just like the sound of being a Martian.

Movies, video games, endless speculations, I've read through the history. Mars colonization was as much a cultural invention of the twentieth century as it was a promise that humanity could avoid its past mistakes, if only we could get a mulligan on the whole planet-species interaction thing. Plus, it's closer to Earth than Venus. So, there's a convenience factor too.

My sister Gloria has been brainwashed into thinking

humans really can eventually thrive there. All those little farms, connected by tubes, earthlings have come to see this as a kind of paradise, though you still can't go outside without an oxygen mask. I think I'd rather choke to death than live in nuclear family-sized glass bubbles for the rest of my life.

As it happens, today marks the forty-ninth anniversary of my life on Venus, largely spent in glass bubbles, floating along in the Venusian atmosphere. The only difference is we never expected this to be paradise. Today's log, I'm told, will be sent to three thousand high schools across Canada. The missive will get there in a year. When I'm about to make my way home.

This exercise is meant to get students excited about space exploration. Why they asked a certified Mars skeptic to share her thoughts is beyond me. I hope they aren't too disappointed.

I guess I'll get right to it. First off, kids, we don't live on the surface of Venus. It's too hot. I and three of our original ten highly trained astronauts are living on enormous floating terra discs, about thirty miles above Venus proper where the atmosphere is thinner, and the temperature is more like the Sahara Desert than a nuclear reactor.

The acid clouds were probably the biggest challenge. In the end, NASA engineers constructed the terra discs with cross-linked polyethylene and over a dozen thrusters on all sides. These thrusters manage to create a sort of hurricane's eye within Venus's heavy winds. We go through a lot of fuel. Personally, I was astonished it all worked. While we've had to get a little creative over the years, each of us I think have had that moment, where we go out onto the disc platform and stare into the maelstrom before us, awed that we are somehow safe from it.

The data we've collected has been similarly awe-inducing, though I can't go into details. It's mostly classified. In short order we scanned the entire planet and then moved on to more detailed findings via probes and our own home-grown experiments. I've become the resident xeno-archaeologist. Rachel Delacroix (France) recently obtained her PhD in geology—specializing in Venusian volcanoes. It was a proud moment for all of us.

Because of the heat, there are few traces of any previous life on the planet's surface, though we've found lots of evidence of prions and a few viruses that would require a host to survive. We have also found some interesting detritus within our cloud ring. Hiroki Saito (Japan) got the idea of rigging up some nets, much like those you would use for bird capture and identification. Putting them up for mere seconds is enough to move us eighty kilometres from our original location, so we don't do it often. The few times we have, we've collected some fascinating data. Highlights include an artificially carved rock, some metallic pieces that could have been part of some tools, and what Adeola Adenekan (Ghana) believes to be fossilized stool samples. Thus far it appears there were fish-like creatures living in the Venusian cloud rings, treating the winds as a kind of endless, vicious current. That at least, is what Adeola has theorized.

We are very familiar with how Venus became the uninhabitable wasteland it is today. In simple terms, it was a combination of being too close to the Sun, and a runaway greenhouse effect. Intense UV rays destroy water molecules. Hospitable planets need water for lots of reasons, but the biggest one is because it carries CO_2 out of the atmosphere into oceans, and eventually the CO_2 finds its way under the planet's outer crust, returning to the atmosphere via volcanoes.

Could a runaway greenhouse effect happen on Earth, you might be asking? Yes. Very easily. The more we pollute the planet, the hotter it gets, and the hotter it gets, the fewer precipitation events we get to capture and store carbon in the oceans and the Earth's crust. That's why I'm here. We know there was once life on Venus. We are trying to figure out how it survived for as long as it did, in case Earth starts looking hotter and drier than it already does. We're also trying to see if there's any way to solve the problem of Venus's noxious, lifeless atmosphere. I'll let you go ahead and guess why.

Our findings up to this point have been inconclusive, the runaway greenhouse effect still irreversible as far as we can tell. Yet Martian scientists busy themselves with encouraging the greenhouse effect and experimenting with man-made magnetic fields in order to eventually oxygenate the atmosphere. Meanwhile we see every day what could happen if it all goes wrong, and we are still, desperately trying to figure out how to reverse it. We are playing God with two gods, of war and love. It's almost poetic.

It's disappointing to say the least that we haven't fulfilled our primary mission objective. I wanted to come back with fewer questions than answers. Around year thirty, I knew this would be impossible. Call it maturing, or perhaps a descent into realism. Our final mission will be to test nanobots Adeola developed that will intake CO_2 and propel themselves forcefully out of the atmosphere to decay in deep space. NASA and the Canadian Space Agency are excited about the possibility of using them on Earth.

We've discussed our concerns about using Venus as a guinea pig for Earth saving schemes many times. Occasionally we've mentioned them to our superiors back on Earth, with little success. It is a shame the only one of us who studied ethics has been dead for almost twenty years. We all wish we had better rebuttals to Houston's willful ignorance.

I tried to take up the cause, but I got stuck in Latin. I fell in love with the language before I could really move on beyond Seneca and Plutarch. Do schools teach you history that far back? Mine didn't. The more I read the more I think they should. It's a lot like archaeology in some ways, because when I read Latin it's like I'm coming to the origins of scientific language and its meanings. What I also love is it shows what might have been, had we chosen to define ourselves differently.

Here's a lesson for you kids. *Homo* is what we know commonly as the origin of the word human. *Caput*, meaning head, or *spiritus* meaning spirit could have also been used to describe humans. Why did we choose one over the others? *Mortalis* is another one once used, meaning mortal which strikes me as deeply ironic, as we make faster strides towards immortality every day. Perhaps we sloughed off *mortalis* for *homo* because even the Romans hoped to move beyond death. *Vita* is apparently a literal translation of life, but the origin of the word "life" itself is most commonly related to the word "body" in old Dutch.

It is easy for me to fall down this rabbit hole now that I am so close to returning to Earth, so apologies to those hoping to get a log entry filled with technical problems and exciting research findings. It feels somehow more significant to be thinking about the words we use when discussing life and human existence while I'm living on a hostile planet, where no humanoid creature has ever lived before us (so we think), where we are forced to separate ourselves from the planet's surface and its toxic air. Incidentally, *animalis*, origin of animal, means "having breath". I think about this most often when I'm putting on my helmet and oxygen tank to go and collect data from my bevy of probes, or to go to Rachel's place for a glass of rehydrated water and some of Hiroki's moonshine gin. This is what interests me now, the mundanities of living. We have made a kind of life here, it's true, but it's a life without breath, without that rare cycle of taking from the world, and then giving back.

We Animals

DESPITE THE DAMAGE CAUSED BY OUR BRIEF AFFAIR, I think the real victim was that dog. You know the one. Or maybe you've already forgotten. You once told me you had short-term memory loss and I thought, "Why do I always find myself with fragile men?"

The dog was of no consequence to anyone, as far as I know. We were on our motorcycles. It was another long day of riding through the country we met in. I was still petrified of killing myself or others. The fuel gauge was broken, the breaks far too close to the throttle. We were on a dirt road coming down into a rundown village. Behind my filmy visor I didn't see them soon enough; a pack of stray puppies harassing a black plastic bag in the middle of the road. I tried to veer, but the dogs were like crows in their stubborn insistence to stay near their quarry. I clipped a blonde one with my front fender. I heard the yelp. I yelled at you to stop. You kept going and I didn't want to lose you, so I kept going too. You had the map. It was only a stray dog, very probably still alive.

II

CHRISTMAS DAY. MY DAD IS SHOWERING. THE TREES IN our backyard are dipped in ice with sugar on top. There is a squirrel above our birdfeeder. He, like all the others that reside in my backyard, is trying to get to the seeds. He's stuck.

The birdfeeder hangs from twisted wires and the squirrel's got his paw caught between them. The birdfeeder is heavy. He pulls and bites, twitches his tail, pausing between frenzied bursts to listen for the warning sounds of something approaching.

I call out to my dad. No answer. I suddenly wonder if he's fallen. He's been feeling dizzy lately. I think about this and I watch the squirrel flail. I'm a sucker for an underdog. The squirrel keeps biting and pulling and ripping. His little paw is bloody.

I put on my boots and head to the garage. I struggle between the dark narrow alley that represents our detached house, sidle to the backyard, holding the ladder above me. The squirrel yanks even harder as I get closer. The drifts of snow make it hard to straighten the ladder. I step up, reach up—

"Don't touch me!" shrieks the squirrel, with all the might of a creature with nothing to lose.

I swear that's what he said. Startled by the cry that I jerk back, hitting the birdfeeder with my arm and its brief release from gravity gives the squirrel his only real chance of escape and he takes it, leaping onto the patio and then scrambling onto a nearby branch. The ladder sags to the side. I fall. I land on our patio tiles and lie there for a long time.

III

WHY DOES IT SEEM SO NATURAL TO ME THAT ELEPHANTS should have graveyards? I expect an elephant procession through the forest or savannah. I can so easily imagine a troupe of them mourning, the murmur of an elephant hymn trembling through their footsteps. They do sing. Elephants are all basses, humming across miles of grassland, broadcasting grief to other elephants while they find twigs and branches and leaves to cover the bodies of their dead. It's been a dream of mine to see elephants, but I would never want to invade such a ceremony. Like going to a stranger's funeral, only worse. Don't look at me that way you know exactly why.

IV

THE COWS THAT DOT THE ALPS IN SWITZERLAND ARE close to sacred. I hear their bells in the morning and in my dreams. They tell me things I never remember the next morning. Cows populate fields around stone chapels, stare you right in the face as you push upwards into the clouds to a mountain pass and they watch you from their precarious ledges as you trudge back down again. They follow the seasons. Moving to higher climes in the summer makes the cheese somehow taste better. The Emmental does taste like dew on grass. It coats your cheeks, lingers, but doesn't stick to your tongue. Old women climb up muddy mountain sides and tell their secrets to sick cows and they get better. There is a prayer you can whisper in every cow's soft ear, asking them to keep watch, keep vigil, keep the mud aerated, the lawns of glaciers well-manicured. Pregnant cows receive wildflower bouquets. They munch on snowbells like alpine queens.

V

AT FOURTEEN YEARS OLD MY SHI-TZU LHASA APSO MOLLY got her first UTI. We only found out because she was leaving little trails of blood up and down the stairs. There were larger dots left on the steps where she took short rests, arthritic and easily confused as she was.

My mom and I spent a sleepless weekend watching her. We carried her white lump of a body down the stairs, out the back door, onto the lawn and back. I know now what it feels like, what she must have felt. The aching and sore back and constant need to pee. The medication is slow to work yet life has to go on. Her symptoms faded by Monday morning, though they were an omen for the patience, caretaking, the dotage the poor thing would soon require.

VI

THE RED-WINGED BLACKBIRDS ARE BACK FOR THE SPRING. It never occurs to me to wonder where they go. One day they're gone, the next they're warbling in the still barren trees that edge the harbourfront. Their song is so distinct, almost an arpeggio, ending in the full-bodied vibrato of the mightiest opera singers. They take over the artificial patch of green space between the water and downtown, swooping low over passers-by if they linger for too long. The flash of red a brief excitement in a sea of otherwise unremarkable avian colours.

I love to watch them. Most people think they're a nuisance. Once, I was sitting on the pier, listening to the blackbirds and the summer folks running or walking their dogs, and I overheard two women remarking that the birds are sometimes shot in the Bahamas for fun, their vibrant red shoulder tufts easy to see in the marshy areas of Bahamian beaches. No tourist wants to be dive-bombed by a bird while tanning in the Caribbean I guess.

I think the whole thing is shameful. But I also killed a raccoon two months ago, so I can't really judge. It bit my dog and tore apart my garbage cans. I smothered the mother and her babies underneath my shed. I closed off all the exits. I didn't want to pay for an exterminator. They suffocated and died.

I Have To Sing

WHEN MY BROTHER WAS TWELVE, HE DEVELOPED AN obsession with parrots. This was the first one, before the turtles, the skinks and then the corn snakes. Using the money he made walking neighbourhood dogs, he bought a blue-fronted amazon parrot one afternoon in April.

"A what?"

"A blue-fronted amazon parrot, Mom. His name is Mario. I got a cage and everything."

Mario was in fact a "she" as Kyle found out at the subsequent vet trip instituted by our parents. He tried a few other names, but nothing stuck. We always returned to Mario.

KYLE WANTED MARIO AROUND ALL THE TIME. HE BROUGHT her to choir rehearsals, thanks to an indulgent teacher, to soccer practice, and board game nights with his friends. I think my parents were hoping Kyle would outgrow Mario within a few weeks. The opposite happened. Kyle refused to leave the house without her. Granted, being forced to leave town and everyone we knew a month after he got her did not exactly help.

Mom worked for some company that did cybersecurity stuff. Maybe. She wasn't allowed to talk about it. One day as we were watching the VR streams, her company's name started popping up. It was being called an Enemy of the State. She came home earlier than usual, saying we were going on a trip.

"Where's Dad?" I asked as I packed clothes into an old backpack.

Mom was stuffing books into a pillowcase.

"He's already on his way, sweetie. He's going to get things ready for us."

"He's already on his way where?"

"Get your clothes please Kyle."

"I'm putting Mario in her cage. I'll do it in a minute."

"Do it now Kyle, Mario can wait."

"Mom don't yell you're scaring her."

"Kyle," she said, dropping the pillowcase, "I will deal with Mario. Go. Now."

"No! Don't touch her!"

Kyle had a special scream when it came to Mario. It was as if some essential part of him was being torn away and he would rather die than let it go. My brother knew something about love and desperation that I had not yet encountered. I had crushes, sure. They made me ache and stay up all night scrolling through their latest casts, but would I attack my own mother for them? Yeah right. In that moment though, it felt like Kyle might. For a parrot.

We left at eleven thirty that night. When I went to text

my friends that I'd be gone for a while, I couldn't find my phone. Mom had buried all our phones in the backyard.

Once we left the city there was nothing except trees and cloudy skies for hours. Mario and Kyle sang to their favourite playlist. I looked out the window, trying to see stars. Mom didn't say anything. At some point I must have fallen asleep because one minute it was pitch dark, the next, the sun was rising.

Eventually Mom turned the car onto a dirt road, barely visible from the highway. We rumbled along the road for maybe half an hour, then turned on to another one, then another, then, when there was barely anything left to drive on, she stopped. We got out of the car and walked into the woods along a narrow path. We came out into a clearing, surrounded by a tight circle of spindly pine trees. I couldn't even see the car.

The cabin looked like it was growing out of the ground. Moss hugged the stone walls and sagging roof. When we arrived, the chimney was smoking.

"Is Dad here?"

"Yes, May. He got here yesterday like I told you."

"Where's his car?"

"It's gone now sweetheart. Don't worry about it."

Dad greeted us at the door. Kyle was bleary-eyed, and Mario was still snoozing on his shoulder. We hauled all our bags inside, found our beds and fell asleep.

The next day we got properly introduced to our new home. The kitchen was ancient, with a deep sink and stained stove that looked like it would have been old fifty years ago. Kyle and I were in one bedroom, our parents occupied a slightly larger one. The toilet did not flush well. There was barely any hot water.

The only interesting feature of the cabin was a trapdoor right by the entrance, covered by a carpet. Once opened, it revealed a kind of dirt cave that held a few crates stuffed with cans and jars. It was almost impossible to see the difference between the trapdoor when it was closed and the rest of the floor. Our parents, after showing it to us, refused to explain how to find it again.

"We go here in case of emergencies. When we tell you to get in, you get in. No arguments."

Besides this rule, we were also told to keep the cabin messy. "As if we've been gone for a while," explained Dad.

It wasn't difficult for me and Kyle, having never been great at keeping up with chores. The smell did start to get annoying though, especially when summer came.

ALL I REALLY WANTED TO DO IN THOSE FIRST WEEKS WAS talk to my friends and find out if they were okay or if they wondered where I was. From the tiny bits I heard on the casts Dad listened to, it sounded like there were lots of Enemies of the State popping up. Eventually Dad stopped listening to the national station and spent hours searching for another cast. When he found one, everyone on it sounded scared. He turned it off every time I tried to listen, so I never really understood what they were saying.

"Don't worry about that. Let's go outside and I'll show you how to make a fire with dry moss."

Our parents often tried to get us outside, collecting water from the creek or finding good birch bark for the fireplace. Neither of us were very outdoorsy. We'd lived in the city our whole lives. My parents had never seemed into nature either yet here they were, chopping wood and scavenging for mushrooms like a pair of wilderness freaks.

Meanwhile, Kyle, Mario and I tried to become ideal outdoorsy kids to please them. This required more time together than I had encouraged over the past few years. Kyle and I had never really been close, our interests veering apart when he became obsessed with animals and truthfully, I could have cared less about Mario. The only problem was we shared a room, so we sort of had to bond to keep things bearable. Dad was teaching me how to play guitar and I would try and accompany Kyle and Mario while they practiced choir music. Eventually Kyle got bored of the same songs over and over, so we started making up our own. Mario would sometimes try to sing along to our unfamiliar words. Other times she'd just mimic the kettle whistle, or branches cracking in the fire.

When we got bored of singing, we'd go outside, often with some chore assigned to us. At first Kyle was terrified Mario would fly away. She had never been in a forest before and I think he assumed she would see it as her ancestral home. I think my parents would have been okay with that to be honest. Mario loved stealing things like pieces of flint, nails or screws. Kyle was constantly worried about how we'd keep feeding her if we couldn't get normal bird food and I could tell it pissed my parents off. Dad used to feed Mario grapes and stuff when we first got her. Now he ignored her as much as possible. He mostly listened to the latest underground casts or went outside to work on the woodshed he was building for the winter. He swore a lot. Mario loved being outside. She didn't fly away despite my parents hopes. I couldn't imagine what Kyle would do if she disappeared. It scared me more than the ominous hum of conversation that filled the house when our parents thought we were asleep.

IT WAS MY IDEA TO TEACH MARIO HOW TO IDENTIFY different trees. One night when Mario and Kyle were asleep, I got up to go to the bathroom and heard our parents talking in their room.

"We have to figure something out. She's too visible. If anyone were to come and look for us, they'd spot her right away."

"If they got close enough to see her, we'd be dead anyway."

"She is a liability Chris, we need to get rid of her."

"What would you tell Kyle? Or May? They're not stupid Scott they'd figure it out."

"Well what do you suggest? I'm not hearing any solutions from you."

We began our tree identification lessons the next day.

Here's what we'd do. We'd go to our new "fort" which was really a pile of misshapen rocks in a convenient circle that offered a bit of seclusion. Then I went to grab different leaves from a variety of trees. Kyle placed them in front of her and together we went over the names of each one.

"Birch, sugar maple, poplar, beech. Okay? You try," said Kyle.

Mario just looked at him.

"It's not working."

"It will, she just needs more practice. Come on let's go over them again."

"Gloria. In excelsis. Deo," sang Mario from her perch on a particularly mossy boulder.

"Shut up Mario."

I started searching for more compelling leaves.

"Don't say that. She's never done this before."

"Yeah well, we're in a crisis situation here Kyle, I'm just

trying to figure out what to do and it's distracting okay?"

"It's not a crisis situation. We're just on…a long vacation."

I stared at him for a minute, wanting to spill every little detail of what I'd heard at night on the casts, the bits of conversation between our parents. More than anything else I wanted to share with my brother how scared I was. I said nothing. I was fifteen and felt like my age meant I could handle certain things that he could not.

"This is stupid," said Kyle eventually, gesturing at Mario to get on his shoulder. "We're going inside."

"Wait. Look, what if we made up a tree song? You stay here. I'll get the guitar. Maybe if we sing about the leaves, she'll start to get it."

"That might work!" said Kyle, on my side once again.

A week later, Mario was flying through the forest bringing back different mosses and strips of bark and had started on mushroom varieties. My parents had started singing her instructions. I stopped hearing about getting rid of Mario.

It felt like the longest summer in history. We ran out of store-bought supplies pretty fast and our parents refused to get more. I couldn't tell if their paranoia was reasonable or not and any time I tried to argue, they always came up with some variant on "you're too young to understand." We made paper. We made traps. Mom taught us how to whittle bows and how to sharpen rocks for arrows. It was all ridiculous. Kyle and I were terrible shots. We absolutely refused to check the traps for dead animals or use leaves as toilet paper. Kyle was oblivious to most stuff that didn't have to do with Mario and I was annoyed because our parents refused to tell us anything important. They got angrier than before if we forgot chores. They yelled more often. They never laughed or joked around with us like they used to. It was like living with strangers.

ON MY SIXTEENTH BIRTHDAY I WAS ORDERED TO GO OUT in the early morning and pick wild strawberries. I didn't know why. I'd given up trying to get my parents to explain anything. Kyle was still asleep, and I wanted to cry at the injustice of it all. It was my birthday. Instead of getting to sleep in and feel normal for once in the last four months, I had to go and pick berries. Maybe I'd get eaten by bears. Mario was also awake. I decided to take her with me.

We went out in the dawn light towards a now well-known berry patch and I tasked Mario with finding twigs for the fire while I foraged.

"I hate my parents," I said to her as she dropped some twigs into an old grocery bag.

"Hate," Mario sang.

"I should run away. Maybe I'll take you and Kyle with me."

"Kyle," she sang louder. "Not run away. Not away."

"Did Kyle try to run away?"

No response. Mario was picking at a strawberry in my basket.

"I wish I had a friend here."

I shooed Mario away from the basket and picked it up, feeling stupid for confiding in her.

"Friend, May. May br-'day."

As soon as we reached our rock fort, I could tell something was wrong at the house. Mario flew off my shoulder towards the cabin singing "Kyle, Kyle, Ave Maria," over and over again. Inside I could hear Kyle going absolutely ballistic. Then my mom threw open the door.

"Where the hell have you been?"

"I was getting berries like you asked," I stammered.

"You've been gone for over an hour we didn't know where you'd gone, and you took Mario without telling Kyle what the hell were you thinking?"

Mom never swore at us. I threw the strawberry basket on the ground. Tiny red jewels scattered across the grass.

"Screw you!" I screamed. "I went and got up when it was still dark out and got your stupid strawberries and all I get is yelled at and it's my birthday and you didn't even remember. I hate you!"

Mom grabbed me by the arm, half-empty basket and bag of twigs in her other hand and dragged me inside. Kyle was in the kitchen, looking worried, Mario on his shoulder. On the counter was a small, carefully decorated cake. The top was ringed with blueberries, with gaps in between them, waiting for a finishing touch.

"S...sorry Mom" said Kyle. "I wouldn't have...I would have been okay if I knew she was with May I just thought she'd gone—"

"That's enough Kyle. We have tried to accommodate you, we have tried to keep you happy, we let you keep that bird but you just...you both refuse to adapt to our situation. You have no idea what your father and I have been through over the past four months," said Mom, still digging her fingers into my arm.

"Yeah we don't," I said, tugging away from her. "Because you never tell us anything. All you do is whisper and turn off the casts when we come inside and never answer our questions. It's like you don't even care about us anymore!"

My throat was burning. Kyle had pushed himself up against the sink, and Mario was squawking intermittently. Mom said nothing. Just stared behind me, out the front door.

"That bird," she said, turning to us again. "Needs to go."

"Mom, please," said Kyle. "Please don't."

She let go of my arm and lunged towards him. He shrieked and crumpled underneath the counter. Mario jumped off his shoulder, flying towards our bedroom.

"Mom, no!"

I grabbed her by the waist and pulled her down to her knees from behind. She twisted and I saw the edge of her face, red with fury. She elbowed me hard in the head. I let go, falling to the floor.

"Oh my God," she said.

Kyle began sobbing.

"Why did you do that?"

My eyes were unfocused. I could see Mom, holding her head in her hands.

"Oh God."

"Chris?"

I turned my head to see Dad at the doorway.

"Chris, they found us we have to go down now."

He paused, as if seeing us all on the floor for the first time. I stared at him, making sure he could see the red swelling on my cheek.

Immediately Mom rose and pulled aside the carpet, sliding her fingers in some secret grooves of wood to open the trapdoor. Kyle followed her down the ladder like a zombie.

"Let's go, let's go," said Dad, who was trying to smoosh cake down the sink.

It was pitch black in the hole. I slid down the dirt wall, trying to calm down. I closed my eyes and felt a hand on mine.

"Are you okay?" whispered Kyle.

I squeezed his shoulder. Then I heard Mom gasp.

"Chris, what is it?" said Dad in a hoarse half whisper.

And then I knew. Kyle knew. I clapped my hand over his mouth.

"Don't," I whispered. "She'll be okay."

"The parrot," said Mom.

"We can't do anything about it now. Why wasn't she with Kyle?"

Dad didn't get an answer because at that moment we heard footsteps overhead. I held Kyle tight against me, trying not to breathe too loud.

"Looks like they're long gone," said a voice.

"There's a parrot in here," said another.

"Gloria. Deo," squawked Mario.

"What's it saying?"

"Don't know. It's singing I think."

"We have to go," she warbled to the tune of Ave Maria. "Let's go, let's go."

"You think they just left it?"

"Run away, run away, May. Popl'r tree."

"Sounds like they've been gone a while. Head out. Search the forest nearby. I'll look for the objective."

Mario started singing Bach's Cantata no. 8, one that she and Kyle had learned right before we'd come here.

"Dumb bird."

For a few moments we could only hear her quiet crooning and a few creaking floorboards. I felt my hand easing over Kyle's mouth. Then, without warning a bang erupted above us. Then silence. Kyle's head was pushed up against my shoulder, his hot tears coursing down my arm. We stayed huddled like that while the men tore through the cabin. They searched for a long time.

WHEN DAD GAVE THE OKAY, WE FINALLY EMERGED. IT was mid-morning the next day. By the look on his face when he saw me it was clear my cheek had swelled up even more. Kyle's face was swollen too, his cheeks and eyelids were covered in tiny red lines, his lips cracked from his salty tears.

It was Mom who went into our room, wrapped Mario in one of her sweaters and brought her outside. Kyle took the shovel and I grabbed my guitar. We dug a hole near our rock fort. By the time we'd finished, the sun was setting. Kyle cradled Mario's body in his arms. We buried her together, patting the dirt down with our hands. As we finished filling the hole, our parents appeared, wary, like they'd cornered a pair of desperate animals.

"We should go kiddos," Dad said.

"We still need to say goodbye," I said, turning away from them. "Go pack or whatever."

"Please guys, look I'm sorry about what happened—"

"Stop," said Kyle. "I have to sing."

He looked at me. Tears still in his eyes, he sang the leaf song we'd made up for Mario.

Our parents stayed in silence, their heads bowed while we sang for Mario, who saved us from a fate we still did not understand.

Bug Eyes

IT TAKES THE CORONER A MOMENT TO REALIZE SHE IS speaking from outside his own mind. The body. The corpse. There were so many maggots when they found her in the park, so many ants eating the maggots. And still she is muttering audibly. Because they found her with no ID in a park, the new one, just built out of the wreckage of an old highway exit ramp, her death was deemed suspicious. He does his job. First the external exam, then internal. Pulls death away to reveal bone. The organs lifted out, carefully now, so the skin can be stitched up again. He bets she killed herself. She looks the type. Too middle class to know that happiness will always be fleeting. He's allowed himself to judge, it's how he keeps her voice at bay. A distracting purr, she mutters rhythmically, soft enough that he can't quite grasp the words. He'd need to move closer to her perfect lips, untouched by the racoons that build homes in all the downtown parks. He does not dare move closer. He doesn't want to know what she's talking about. For as long as possible. Eventually, he recognizes an accounting at play. Her voice, lower than he would have guessed, enumerates the last moments before they found her. Each piece of flesh the police didn't recover. Half a fingernail, strands of hair pulled off by wandering squirrels, the upper dermis of her pinky toe, nibbled off by a rat. Blood and tissue gone somewhere, who knows where, becoming part of the vast city landscape.

She was wearing sandals with no grip and regrets them, she whispers. Now, in death, she wishes she'd put on sneakers. Now she begins to recite all that she should have done, what she should have worn. Her list loops on. It's unbearable.

The police don't have a clue, he hears her moan. The coroner is puzzling over something on her ankle. More vital, she claims, is the blood that once oozed from what look like animal scratches, the blood that's now hiding in a single Hister beetle who gnawed on her neck for hours before disappearing into the night.

The truth is, he thinks, she's watched too many cop shows in her short life. He goes home knowing there will be no hero for this girl, this barely-adult who had a beautiful body and a round, young face. He has met his fair share of bodies. They were rarely so lovely, though much more serene in death. Would she insist until all avenues were pursued? Would she whisper from the cold chamber, infecting every one of his subsequent autopsies? God, he thinks. I fucking hope not.

The morgue is silent when he arrives the next day. Moments later, as if she knows he's there, she starts to speak again, her low tone mimicking the freezer's constant drone tumbling through the room.

He doesn't want to go to her, though cause of death is still unknown, and parents may come in today, if the police can find them. He doesn't want to see the results for her inevitably scarred liver but no smoking gun. He will tell the detectives about the approximate time of death, and factors such as decay and weather and drugs. They will sigh and go on asking witnesses the usual questions until a name can be established. His hands are clean, metaphorically speaking. He's done all he can. Still, that afternoon he'll bring her out and notice under the ragged fingernails more maggots trying to break past the skin. Normally, he'd leave them be, they have a part to play in her eventual biodegradation, at least, if she isn't cremated. The murmurs are pleading. They've changed from lists to questions, endless questions. The kind he cannot answer. He scrapes the maggots away and circles back to the nape of her neck, washing her hair, massaging her scalp. She goes quiet. From top to bottom he searches for other signs that nature is taking over. Erases them. For a little longer.

Marla's Ashes

ELLEN'S PARENTS WERE STAYING TOGETHER FOR THE dog. In a long and frankly awkward conversation, her dad explained that Marla—miniature labradoodle, aged thirteen—would never adjust to moving between two new apartments. She frequently cried even when they were sitting in separate rooms.

"So, you're being held hostage by a dog."

"No, we're not. We've been unhappy for a long time, we just figured, what's another six months? She won't be with us much longer."

"How long is a long time?"

Greg held his chin in his hand. They were sitting in his favourite café, a local spot that used to show his photographs when he was starting out. Ellen worked here now, as their bookkeeper. Greg made the introductions after her breakup and subsequent return to the city.

"Let's not do this, okay?"

This told her nothing.

MARLA HAD INVADED THEIR FAMILY WHEN ELLEN WAS eleven. Her mom, Hannah, not at all the spontaneous type, saw Marla in a pet shop window and bought her for five hundred dollars on the spot. It was November, when the city darkened and seemed to hunch in on itself, and it also happened to be the month of her brother Max's seventeenth birthday. Hannah said Marla was for him, "a reason to come back and visit" from school next year. They all knew the dog was for her. A replacement of sorts.

Ellen was immediately jealous of Marla. She got all the attention Ellen had so looked forward to when Max finally left. Her dislike of her brother's dreamy art kid attitude was well documented. Now, when she was about to step onto center stage, Marla had come in to take her place.

Were you unhappy when we were kids?" Ellen asked as Greg got up to leave.

"No, I don't think so. Things were good for a while El. And then they just weren't anymore."

"CAN YOU BELIEVE IT?"

Ellen was having dinner with Max that night. Since coming back to Toronto, she tried to make an effort to keep in touch. Not that he really noticed.

"Yeah actually, I totally can," he said, searing pork chops.

"It's insane. Why take another year of misery just for the dog? They're obsessed with her."

"Mom and Dad are the most passive people I've ever

met. I bet the dog's more of an excuse than an actual reason."

"Max, they left my graduation early because of the dog. It's definitely genuine."

"To be fair, it did sound like she was shitting everywhere. They came back after," he paused. "What, you think they love Marla more than us?"

"More than me anyway." Max laughed.

"Talk about a pity party. You ended up alright in the end."

"Does twenty-five, broke and single sound good to you?"

"No, you're right you're a Greek tragedy. Might as well lay down and die right now. Dinner's ready."

Max dished out the pork chops and some green beans. The kitchen was in a corner at the back of the apartment, with barely any room for a table. They took their plates to the porch and watched some kids playing soccer in the street. Every once in a while the kids would wail "car!" and run to their respective driveways.

"Did you ever notice them fighting or anything?" Ellen asked, finishing off her glass of wine.

"No. I got out of there pretty fast. Wasn't exactly interested in their problems."

"I guess not."

"You ever get a sense of it?"

"I don't know. Some ways yes, when I think about it now. By the time I was leaving for school they were barely speaking to each other. I thought it was like, true love telepathy or something. Wasn't until I started doing the same thing with Marcus that I realized it might have been more like apathy. Like no anger there, just complete indifference."

"That's depressing."

"Yup."

They watched the soccer game for a little while longer. Max cheered loudly whenever someone scored a goal. It made Ellen laugh.

Ellen walked home the long way up Roncesvalles, pausing to look at the shop windows. She and Marcus had been together for six years. Met at the video rental store that sold ice cream down the street. They'd both ordered rocky road. She used to love telling the story.

Marcus was her first love, her only sexual partner, and his family lived two blocks from hers. After six years she thought she was ready to get married. She'd started lingering by the magazine racks at drugstores, perusing the bridal section, too embarrassed to look online in case Marcus caught a peak over her shoulder. Then, shortly after they'd graduated Marcus got a job in Calgary. So, she went with him and they bought a house together. A few months later, Ellen glanced at Marcus's phone and was greeted by a detailed description of what Marcus could have been doing with "Nasty Law Chick" instead of eating dinner with his girlfriend. She threw his phone at the wall and bought a plane ticket the next day. It wasn't like things had been perfect. She just thought he'd respect her enough to break it off before moving on to someone else. Maybe he needed a better reason to end things than simply being unhappy.

A WEEK AFTER HER DAD DROPPED THE NEWS ABOUT THE divorce, Ellen was standing in front of her parent's house. It had three stories, with dainty filigree awnings and was wedged between two other gothic nightmares in the midst of being flipped. The house all tight spaces and narrow hallways, and filled with dust both her parents ignored. Its only saving grace was the garden, which ended in a graceful willow tree.

"When you guys retire, you think you'll sell this place?" Ellen said as she opened the screen door and joined her parents on the back porch.

Her parents were sitting in matching Adirondack chairs, Marla fussing in Hannah's lap.

"Can't retire from art," said Greg.

"About that time anyway for me though," said Hannah.

"I was mostly joking."

"Well, my department is changed a bit lately. Not sure I like the direction it's going. But we won't be selling the house at least until…" she trailed off, glancing down at Marla, whose head was lifted with some effort to mark Ellen's arrival.

"Would you mind getting the wine from the fridge El?"

Ellen went inside, and instead of searching for the wine in her parent's overstuffed fridge, she wandered through the house. Nothing looked out of place. It didn't look as though they'd started packing or dividing things up. She went upstairs expecting to see her room or Max's room being used. No. They were still sleeping in the same bed. She came back outside, wine in hand.

"Glasses El?" said Greg.

"Look did I mishear or are you not in fact getting divorced?

They looked at each other. Her mom sighed.

"We are. I thought you and your father had already talked about it."

"Yeah we did. But if you looked around the house you would have no idea. You're still sharing a bed?"

"Bit personal, El," said Greg. "Can you get the glasses

please?"

"We're in the middle of a conversation," said Ellen, hurrying inside and returning with three wine glasses.

"Five El, Max's coming with Irina."

"You couldn't have mentioned that before?" Ellen muttered.

"Now Ellen," quavered Hannah.

She did that. Her voice went high whenever she didn't like something. It was as close as she ever came to yelling.

"I just, I don't understand guys, you're not acting like a couple divorcing."

"Well we both sleep better in the same bed. And Marla is up and down all night if I try to sleep in another room," said Hannah.

"Are you serious?"

"It's easier this way."

Ellen could hear Max at the door. Irina calling out hellos.

"Help me get dinner set up El?" said Greg, getting out of his chair.

"I'll bring the wine back in," said Hannah.

And now it was Ellen's fault the evening felt awkward, the conversations stilted. She chopped potatoes with her dad in silence, while Irina tried to make conversation with her mom outside. Hannah wasn't paying attention, so Max was taking over her side while she stroked Marla who was falling asleep.

"Are you seeing anyone Ellen?" Irina asked at dinner.

They were eating red quinoa with onions, peas and cashews, alongside a "super food" salad Greg had found on a website he claimed to now frequent regularly. It was all about eating right for seniors. Ellen thought it was morbid.

"Not at the moment. Everything still feels a bit raw, you know?"

Irina nodded. She was an actor who specialized in Francophone puppetry. She'd been trying to convince Max for over a year now to move to Montreal even though Max doesn't speak French. He's not even very good at learning it. They will break up, thinks Ellen, and then feels terrible for thinking it.

"It's been almost six months El, I figured you would have given dating a try at this point," said her dad.

"We were together for a long time Dad. You know they say that after a breakup the mourning period can last for like, half the time you've been together."

"Are you saying you're not going to date for the next three years?"

"Maybe you're too old to remember your first love Greg," Irina teased. "It hurts the most the first time, I think."

"More wine anyone?" said Hannah.

"I don't think that's true," said Greg. "I think Ellen tends to focus on the negative. Why not remember the good times you had and move on?"

"How can you say that? It's not that simple. He cheated on me. I'm still processing."

"Dickbag," said Max.

"Thank you, Max."

"Come on El."

Greg was getting up, taking everyone's plates and putting them in the dishwasher.

"You really thought you were going to be with Marcus the rest of your life? You were so young when the two of you met, I mean people break up all the time at your age. Personally, I was hoping you'd ditch him in Calgary, start a life of your own."

"News to me, I thought you liked him."

"He was fine. You were both kids. I didn't think it would last."

Ellen could feel herself tensing. She could barely stomach the bland quinoa and smelly salad anymore. She wanted to go home, wanted someone who could comfort her, knowing that her apartment held only a box of crackers, peanut butter and mice. She didn't even own a bedframe.

"You're getting divorced so I don't know if you have any right to be telling me what I should or shouldn't have done in my relationship."

Irina let out a little gasp.

"Good one El," said Max.

"Red wine with dessert I think, right?" said Hannah.

DESSERT IN THE LIVING ROOM WAS UNSURPRISINGLY tense. Ellen was already on her second helping of strawberries and cream, still hungry from the lacklustre dinner. Max was talking about his latest project, a teen drama about exchange students in Toronto. He was doing the art direction.

"I think this one might put me in touch with some people from England. It'd be great to get into one of those twenty year running cop shows the Brits seem to be crazy about. Like, my Coronation Street."

"Is that really what you want Max?" said Greg. "Working on some British soap opera for easy cash? Where's your artist's vision?"

"It's buried in my artist's debt."

Irina laughed, eating the whipped cream around the strawberries.

"At least he's making a living," said Hannah. "That's the

most important thing."

"If he wants to be an artist, he shouldn't be selling out so young."

"Dad, you did commercial photography for years before you made any money as an artist," said Ellen. "Since when did you decide you were the arbiter of all that is good and true?"

"There's no need to be so dramatic," huffed Greg. "I'm just saying that Max has a talent I had to work at for years. He shouldn't waste it."

"I'm not wasting it, I'm paying rent."

"Can we all stop bickering please," said Hannah. "I hate it when you three argue. Ellen. Come take the dog out for a walk please. The rest of you can clean up. Change the subject."

MARLA WAS NOT PLEASED TO BE GOING OUT. IT WAS A humid evening and the mosquitoes were out in abundance. They danced around Marla's shaggy head as she dawdled behind Ellen and Hannah, who were coaxing her into making it around the block.

"Ellen, please don't be so hard on your father when we get back," said Hannah. Marla arthritically squatted to pee.

"What's his problem anyway? It's like he was trying to pick a fight with us. I wasn't the one who brought up Marcus."

"He's feeling a bit jaded at the moment sweetheart. He's become very aware that he's on his final decades of life."

"Not very fair to resent his kids for that."

"He doesn't resent you."

They were barely walking anymore, Marla was waddling ahead of them, ready to get out of the heat.

"He...he's not doing well with what's going on."

"What do you mean?"

"About the divorce Ellen."

"I thought that was mutual. He sort of made it sound like you'd both decided this."

"Well no. That's not exactly how it happened."

They walked for a few more blocks before rounding the corner back onto their street.

"Mom why are you staying?"

"It's Marla, Ellen. She's not going to be around much longer. I'd miss her too much if I left now."

"She's a dog mom. We're talking about your life here."

"Ellen this is my life," said Hannah. They were almost back at the house now, almost at the front steps.

"I haven't known a different life for almost thirty years. I know you think that your breakup with Marcus was devastating and you'll never get over it, but six years is a drop in the bucket. This is my best friend I've fallen out of love with. I'm trying to make it as easy on him as possible. On all three of us."

"What all three of you. The dog?"

"Yes, the dog," snapped Hannah.

"She's old and she's dying and it's the least we can do for her. It would all just confuse and upset her."

Ellen opened the door and her mom picked up Marla and carried her inside.

ELLEN WOKE UP EARLY ON SATURDAY AND WENT FOR A run. Her mom had asked her to come by sometime in the next week to "discreetly" start going through all her childhood things. She'd asked Max to do the same. "On a different day than your brother though, okay?"

She wondered how much her father knew about it. Or whether he was burying his head in the sand, as he sometimes did when information sprang up he did not want to hear.

She was running east, towards downtown before circling back down south to come up along the Humber. It was a long route. She'd gotten into running because Marcus liked it. She ran her first race with him. When they moved to Calgary, he said he'd lost interest, preferred going to the gym. Now it was hers at least, she didn't have to feel like it was some part of her personality she'd only borrowed from him.

Her thoughts returned to her dad. When Max had come home after second year and announced in his gentle, matter-of-fact way that he was bisexual, Greg just nodded and then asked Max to help him with a crossword puzzle. Max took it as tacit acceptance. Ellen could tell her dad was actively trying to forget the whole thing. Max hadn't brought a guy home yet to force the memory back up. Ellen sometimes wondered why.

Hannah of course had accepted it with joy.

"We're so happy for you," she'd said, "so glad you told us."

The same thing happened when Marla was diagnosed with cancer a year ago. A tumour on her leg. It could be removed, though the doctors doubted she'd survive the surgery. She was old, they said. It was inevitable. All they could do was ease her pain.

Ellen hadn't even heard until she was telling Hannah about her decision to come back home.

"You didn't know? Your father told me he was going to let you know."

But he hadn't.

Her mom shrugged it off as forgetfulness. Thing was, she refused to nag him. She always said if he couldn't remember something, like the grocery list, to do laundry, to call his daughter, well she wasn't his personal secretary.

And yet Ellen couldn't let that stuff go and had no aversion to conflict. She was like Greg that way, always ready for an argument. Her mom was just as likely to leave the room when they started arguing. Ellen wasn't very up on politics but she read the news just so she could shut her dad up. She rarely beat him in an argument unless it was about taxes. He tended to steer clear of that topic.

These arguments always felt like a test. With Marcus, she'd usually agreed with him because she thought that was what good couples did. As she made her way down to the Lakeshore she wondered now if he'd suggested Calgary as his last-ditch effort to have an argument that would end in them breaking up, end in her finally admitting she said yes to most things to keep him around. Not out of love, but out of fear of being without him. The thought made her heart pound. She slowed down and hobbled towards a bench, heaving, trying not to cry in front of strangers.

ON MONDAY, ELLEN LEFT WORK A BIT EARLY AND WALKED down King street to Marla's vet clinic. Marla had an overnight checkup and Hannah was out late for some colloquium talk and Greg was scheduled to set up a gallery in the Beaches for his latest show. He wouldn't tell them what it was about. "There's no surprise in life anymore!" he said when they pestered him.

Marla was suffering, the vet said.

"She has arthritis in her back legs and the tumor makes

it difficult for her to walk. We can't know for sure where else the cancer's spread without a number of x-rays. I know it's not easy to hear, but I would recommend putting her down before her quality of life deteriorates any more."

"Okay," said Ellen. "I'll talk to my parents about it."

"They know the drill unfortunately. Marla's been here a lot over the last few months."

Ellen thanked the vet and put Marla's leash on. She felt awful making her walk after what the vet said, who was cute and was watching them leave, so she picked her up. Marla barely weighed anything.

"Jesus, Marla," said Ellen as she carried her down the street. "What are they going to do about you?"

When they got home, Marla flat out refused to go out again, so Ellen opened the screen door and let her stumble around in the backyard. With every step she took Ellen could hear the vet's words. It was torture watching her move around like that.

Eventually they were both on the couch—Ellen having boosted Marla up because she could no longer get any traction on the floor—and were watching trashy TV. Marla's head was on her leg and she kept on heaving long doggy sighs, as if disappointed in the life choices of the contestants on America's Next Top Model.

"Don't judge," said Ellen, rubbing Marla's head.

"Hello?"

"Hi Mom," said Ellen, turning off the TV.

"Good talk?

"It was wonderful, yes. Not every day you get Thomas Piketty speaking at your university. The students were going crazy over him."

"I bet."

Ellen pulled her leg out from underneath Marla's head and got up to get a glass of water.

"How was the vet?"

"It was okay."

Hannah came and sat next to Marla, stroking her back while she snored.

"The vet recommends she be put down Mom."

"I know he does."

"He says she's in a lot of pain. He gave me some pills, but he says they're not really going to do much."

"Right. Okay. I thought we had a bit more time," said Hannah, now bent over, kissing Marla's head.

"I'll talk to your father about it."

Ellen nodded, then came over and hugged her mom, careful not to jostle the couch too much, so as not to wake up Marla.

THE APPOINTMENT WAS SCHEDULED FOR THE FOLLOWING Monday. Ellen hadn't seen her dad all week. When she went to sort through her things, he was apparently at the gallery again.

"He's getting a handle on everything," said Hannah.

Ellen formed piles to give away and to keep. In one of her old desk drawers she found a couple of photos of when she'd had her own photography phase, mostly just to hang out with her dad, and Greg had taught her everything with an endearing intensity. The photo was of the two of them, eyes glued to the camera viewer, trying to take macro shots of wildflowers in the front yard. Her mom had captured the memory. What would he do without her? Who would be there to capture memories for him? It struck her then that she really knew nothing about her parents' relationship. Not what they fought about or what they shared. How did you fall out of love with someone? She had never been in love before Marcus and had never asked him why his feelings had changed. When had her mom known they weren't right for each other anymore? She wasn't about to ask her. It seemed too depressing to bring up.

WHEN THE TIME CAME, ELLEN MET MAX AT HIS PLACE, and they walked together to the vet. She hadn't really wanted to come. Hadn't wanted to share Marla's last moments.

"I wasn't exactly her number one fan."

"Please Ellen. It would mean a lot to us if you were both there. She's like your sister," said Hannah.

"Once, again, she's a dog."

But Ellen wasn't really up to arguing about it. When she and Max got to the vet's they were taken to a room where their parents were already sitting down on the floor, giving Marla treats.

It was very peaceful. There was the sedative, and then the shot of whatever it was that did the job, and then, well she just sort of fell asleep, cradled in Hannah's arms. They were all crying. Greg was crying a little harder than everyone else. The vet kept saying to him "she's not in any pain anymore." Of course he knew that, thought Ellen. A life was ending. It was as simple as that.

The Fox

IT IS CUSTOMARY AT THE BLUE MONKEY CAFÉ TO introduce newbies to the back alley on their first day of work. Right before close, the newest barista is piled high with garbage and told to navigate between the café and an office furniture store. It's a thin space that offers up such obstacles as black ice, pigeon shit and the occasional modern-art splatter of Friday night puke. If you get to the dumpster and back with no injuries, you're officially part of the team.

The café has faux-leather chairs, slightly tinted windows so as to avoid glare on laptop screens and cardamom in its lattés. There are more alternative milk options than you can count, but the dumpster is still a dumpster, same as anywhere else: really, really gross.

Worse, right before I started the owner decided to institute composting. It's the beginning of March. The city's vermin can smell the rotting food, no matter how animal proof the containers claim to be.

"I heard Mel saw a huge raccoon a couple of weeks ago just waiting for her to drop the compost bag," says Corey, thirty-three, café veteran and hellbent on becoming an opera singer.

"I bet it was just a huge rat," says Tom, twenty-three, aspiring makeup artist to the stars, sidling into the cramped breakroom to punch in for the day.

"Mel's always full of crap."

"Have you guys ever seen anything back there?" I ask.

"I mean, mice for sure," says Corey, immediately authoritative.

"Cockroaches in the summer, but that's everywhere. Honestly, there's a McDonalds like a block away that I know for a fact throws all its food in the dumpster. They've got way bigger problems than we do."

"Famous last words!" sings Tom, donning his apron.

Mel never told me about any raccoon encounters. In the three weeks I've been here we'd gotten pretty close, in the sense that I pester her about her life, and she mostly obliges. I'm a bit hurt, though it helps me understand a few things about Mel. For one, whenever we are on shifts together, I am always on garbage duty.

Most people don't aspire to work in coffee shops. For me, it's an ideal situation. Flexible hours, easy work and free coffee. I just moved to Toronto. I'm working on a screenplay, doing auditions on the side. Our boss Tanya is a bit of a hippie and doesn't care too much if you dip out early. To be honest she's a total space cadet. I'm already thinking of ways to integrate her into my screenplay.

ON TUESDAY MORNINGS I OPEN THE CAFÉ. I WAKE UP, grab jeans and my black work t-shirt (with the outline of a blue monkey on it, it's cool so I'm definitely keeping it when I quit) and slouch my way to the kitchen.

My roommate is already there, prepping for an audition. Lara told me about it last week and asked me not to go to the casting call. I could easily get the role she so obviously wants. It's some artsy experimental stage production. I'm not interested. Lara's dad is in the business and is basically her agent. He sends her these long lists of open calls and auditions every week. Occasionally I take a peek at her phone, and if there's something interesting I tell him (as Lara) to send the details. That way I don't need to pay for an agent, and Lara's dad thinks his daughter's well on her way to doing some actual money-making acting, instead of the broke artist shit she's currently in love with.

You're up early," I say. Lara doesn't usually emerge from her room until at least lunch.

"My call time is like, eight-thirty. Alex is killing me. He wants us to do the read through this morning, then come back at midnight for some kind of bonding exercise."

It's cute watching Lara try to be exasperated with Alex. She is one hundred percent in love with him. If he's not in my kitchen eating my cheerios by the time previews roll around, I'll eat Lara's script.

"You getting paid for that?" I ask.

Lara rolls her eyes, again, like she doesn't want to spend all night "bonding" with that turd.

"No. Of course not."

I make some toast and get out before she starts complaining more about a man she would probably learn rudimentary Mandarin for if he asked. Not even if he asked, if he implied it would be cool. Sometimes I really want to shake Lara. The impulse always passes. I've got a first-row ticket to the reality show that is her life. It's great.

The thing I like the most about the Blue Monkey is that it doesn't pretend to be Starbucks or any other chain coffee shop. We open at eight and don't care if some tight-ass banker can't get his coffee in time for the morning meeting. We get all the artists and freelancers and that's just fine with me because they are fodder for my screenplay, among other things.

I'm opening with Mel today (twenty-seven, from Saskatchewan, smokes like she's trying to forget something). I'm still thinking about Mel's raccoon run-in, because I think it would also be useful for my screenplay. I am always thinking about my craft.

I'm writing a screenplay for a kid's show about life in the city. Lara's dad just happens to know someone at TVO and may or may not think his daughter is busy at work on this great idea for an animated series. I want kids to know about all the crazy stuff that happens in cities in a non-scary way. Well, non-terrifying way. It's not fun if you can't scare them a little bit. Kid's stuff can be pretty lucrative if it works out. Mostly because no one wants to get stuck in toddler world the rest of their career. Their loss. I like kid's stuff because you can say things that shock adults and go right over kids' heads, but they laugh anyway. A double whammy. And sometimes kids do get the adult stuff. Which is even better.

Anyway, this raccoon thing could be good. A kid has to take out the garbage and then all of the sudden there's a bunch of raccoons hanging out in his backyard! There'd be some kind of lesson in it. Like, how raccoons are people too or something. Or the raccoons eat the kid and the lesson is, stay away from raccoons, they'll eat you.

"Hey Mel, Corey told me you saw a huge raccoon in the back alley."

"Yeah when I was closing," says Mel, who is putting beans in the espresso machine.

"What did it look like? Like was it really that huge? Did its eyes look bright red?"

"It was just a raccoon. Nothing special. It just freaked me out when it popped out from behind the dumpster."

"Okay yeah, but look I'm trying to write an episode for my screenplay about a kid and some raccoons, and I've never actually seen one. So, what did it look like?"

"You've never seen a raccoon?"

"No, they don't hang around that much in Sudbury. Everyone tells me they're all over the place here."

"So find a YouTube video or something."

"But I want the narrative drama! What did it feel like when it spooked you? What did you think it was at first?"

I know it might seem like I'm pushing it. Mel is not an overly talkative gal. We talk about dumb sitcoms we both watch and gossip about Corey being a slut. This is the first time it feels like we're talking about something real. A raccoon attack, I mean come on! Real enough to make a kid understand the surreal challenge of sharing this vast planet with millions of other complex, living, breathing creatures. Or something like that.

"I don't want to talk about it okay?"

"But why?" I whine. "It'll be such great background for my episode, it would be so helpful, and I want to be ready if I see one back there myself."

"It wasn't a raccoon okay!"

Mel is furiously grabbing muffins from the fridge, squishing the tops, and stomping to the display case to stuff them in, deformed. I don't know what to say. This just makes the story all the more intriguing. How could she not know that?

"What do you mean?"

Mel stops her muffin grabbing and stuffing and pulls me into the back room, face inches from mine.

"It wasn't a raccoon it was a guy behind the dumpster okay now leave me the fuck alone before I fucking fire you," she whisper-yells at me.

She really can fire me. She's assistant manager.

"Guys what is going on?"

Tom, dazed pre-coffee, hair in a high pouffe looking not unlike a young Jim Carrey, enters the café.

"Nothing. Is going. On." Mel says through clenched teeth.

She grabs the rest of the muffins and storms off.

"Get your aprons on."

"She's in a mood," says Tom.

I love Tom if only because he is a sucker for drama and man is it fun to make him try and pull it out of you. The problem for him is, I like keeping secrets more than sharing them.

I just smile and go out to man the cash. So not raccoons. A random dude. Who may or may not have given Mel a little more than a surprise. We can't put that in a kid's show now can we.

I LIKE MYSTERIES AS MUCH AS THE NEXT PERSON. MY mom read them like an addict. If she didn't have Hercule Poirot, John Rebus, or if in dire straits, good ol' Sherlock by her side, then she was pissy all day. My mom was a "homemaker", which means she mostly read and screeched at me to turn the TV down or get dinner started. When I was finally interested in reading recreationally, they were the only thing on the shelves. So yeah, I know how a good mystery goes.

Even if I'm writing for kids, I always try to add a little inquiry into the mix, because kids can be smart sometimes. The kid in this current episode, for example, doesn't realize the raccoons in his backyard are raccoons at first. At first, he thinks they're little monsters or something. Little creepy gremlins. But then, he investigates and realizes the raccoons just sound scary and are fatter than he thought. Adults, they want to believe in monsters, because they're lives are so damn boring. Kids, on the other hand, need a little more reality in their lives, and mystery provides them with a helpful reminder that most questions have logical answers. Ultimately, besides the potential for a huge payout, that's why I like writing for them. They're gullible, but also curious. Like dumb cats. While not the worthiest opponents, I like playing tricks on kids. They are more likely to laugh afterwards than threaten to sue.

The story of the man behind the dumpster would have to fit into something else. As I make small talk with customers, quickly writing down what they look like in my phone for inspiration (cosplay chick, green hair, lip piercing, good for an episode about drag queens?) I keep watching Mel out of the corner of my eye. Waiting to see if her actions will reveal anything more about the incident.

The thing is, the Blue Monkey is the kind of place that might have homeless dudes in the back alley, or drunk ravers, or one of Tanya's boytoys masturbating. It could have been a young filmmaker, drunk off his ass from celebrating the end of filming, taking a piss when Mel walked out and scared the bejeezus out of him. We are just north of the film district, after all.

Multiple suspects, multiple motives—maybe Mel had an even more compelling reason to be out in the alley than taking out the garbage—it was delicious stuff for a writer/actor such as myself. Mel hadn't even looked at me since our exchange that morning. I wasn't going to learn more from her. I need to get creative.

Corey calls in sick which means he was either at an audition, getting ready for an audition or found someone to have sex with him. So, I tell Tanya I'll take the afternoon shift if I can go to a callback at lunch.

"You are just so my saviour today hun, I so, so appreciate it," says Tanya, Mel shooting daggers at me behind Tanya's back.

I couldn't care less. I'll be closing, which means I can take out the garbage and keep my eyes out for miscreants to be my muses.

THE CALL IS FOR THIN BLONDES IN THEIR TWENTIES. IT IS generic horror movie fare. Girl gets killed off in the first fifteen. I am probably the two-hundred-and-thirty-seventh girl to go into the windowless audition room. The casting director looks like she is about to slit her wrists.

I read some lines and five minutes later the casting director thanks me. They all get up and stretch. I walk out into the hallway. As I put my jacket on, one of the producers comes out of the room.

"We're about to have our lunch break, you want something from catering?"

"What do they have?"

"Good stuff. Some idiot's putting a lot of money into

this production," he says, rolling his eyes in a way that I'm sure he thought was playful.

"Sure, sounds great."

I follow him through a couple of doors, watching the others go the complete opposite way, until we come to what is clearly his office. Subtle.

There are only so many times you can be asked what you're willing to do to get a part before your response becomes a swift knee to the asker's groin and then sauntering off as if nothing happened. I'm not a vigilante. I just love a punchline the audience doesn't expect. It's another kind of trick I enjoy. I get back to the Monkey a little early and get started mixing our chai blend.

"How did it go?" asks Tom.

"Great. I think I definitely have a shot. They're posting the notice tomorrow."

"Oh my god that's awesome. You are such a hustler, I wish I could do what you do."

"Tom isn't Keon working in film right now? Call him up and get some work."

"No way. He was trash. I'm not talking to that ass ever again."

I shrug. Tom bounces back to Keon with the puppy dog eyes about once a month. He could at least get something out of it.

"You're late," says Mel when I come out with the chai.

"Nope, I'm not, you were just busy when I came in."

"Whatever."

The rest of the afternoon is pretty boring except I am able to get some valuable raccoon info from a grad student who is moping around on a bar stool. He works in conservation and asks for my number, so I promptly give him

Mel's. He seems eager to please. She could probably use some positive male interaction.

At closing Mel leaves without even asking me to take out the garbage like she usually does. Like it's implied that it's always going to be my job now.

"Okay seriously what is her problem?" asks Tom, who is pretending to sweep the floors.

"She got jumped. In the alley."

"What. No. Oh my god we have to call the police or something. We have to tell Tanya."

"Tom, you know what? I'll tell Tanya. Why don't you head out early. This has been really weighing on me all day," I say, hand on my chest like I'm saying the pledge of allegiance.

"I'd rather be the one to tell her."

"I can't let you stay here by yourself, after what you just told me."

"I'll be fine. Look you should definitely go because I know for a fact that there's this amazing new spa place in Yorkville that's having an opening thing, and they're doing this beauty and makeup contest where you can just walk off the street and show them you're stuff, and you should definitely go!" I say, like I just remembered.

"Are you serious right now? Why didn't you tell me this earlier?"

Tom is running to the back now, gets his coat, drops the broom on the floor and throws his plastic gloves in the garbage. I didn't tell him until now, because it didn't exist until now. I'm not worried, these things work themselves out. There is a new spa that just opened in Yorkville, who's to say they don't do interviews by contest?

"I mean I thought you knew because Keon is going..."

"Oh of course he's going. No, he will not take another job from me."

Tom is out the door ten seconds later. I have the place to myself. I wait until all of Tanya's friends have stopped banging on the door, hoping to get sauced on her dime. I do a deep clean of the fridges and freezers because I'm feeling generous. Three weeks in and the Blue Monkey is inspiring all kinds of great story ideas. It makes me want to stop everything, go home and ask Lara's dad if he knows anyone at Netflix.

Instead, I clean the espresso machine. I scrub down the toilets with ice cold water because it makes me smile knowing the first person in tomorrow will do a little jump off the toilet seat and maybe even scream. I even refill the whip cream canisters. Model employee.

Close to one in the morning, I get the garbage together and go to the back alley practically vibrating with excitement. The truth is, I have a soft spot for scavengers, and if it was just some homeless dude, I might pivot my story, ask him about his life. Write some HBO-style thing about a homeless anti-hero. If it does turn out to be a straight up rapist, that will require a different approach. Possibly one that is a bit more fun.

As I am hauling out the bags, my phone buzzes. A text message from Lara.

"Are you sleeping with ALEX?"

Oh Lara. One day you'll thank me.

I throw my bags into the dumpster and that's when I notice a shape leaning its arms on the Office Depot wall. It's a man alright, but is he our mystery man? I move into the shadows by the door. He appears to be puking. He is wearing a tie. It's loose around his collar. His hair is mussed up and looks greasy. He looks like he no longer belongs in his bespoke suit. I have this image suddenly, of me telling this story to a stand-up audience. Should I start doing stand-up? I file this away for later.

I watch him for a little longer. He stops puking and turns to put his back on the wall. As he moves in the dim streetlight, I notice another figure, slumped on the other side of him, in a tight pink dress. Her feet look so awkward, splayed on the ground in some four-inch heels.

My favourite kind of trick is the kind that breaks the rules. There's nothing funnier than a terrified man.

Slowly, as I move out of the shadows, I can't help but smile so wide that I might look, at first glance, like I'm baring my teeth. I stifle a giggle, thinking about how I will tell this story later. TV? A film deal? Maybe I'll get into podcasting. All minor details. I know I'm going to kill.

C a l l   M y   C a t s

IT WAS IN THE EARLY DAYS OF THE PANDEMIC, WHEN ALL we did was take long walks around town. No, we were not New York. Fear clung to us all the same. We slept like the dead and were tired the next day. I was finishing up teaching a comparative Canadian literature class when it started. I felt like a zombie. The students noticed. One emailed me asking if everything was okay.

Most days Colin and I would manage to go for a walk. Usually it was around noon, when we could justify a long lunch. The streets were dead. We liked to walk through the Glebe, a neighbourhood filled with abandoned mansions. It was south of our gentrifying block, easy to get to. Often, we'd continue south until we hit the canal, then follow it around towards the golden triangle. Another rich part of town.

The birds sang and danced through the streets. There were no cars to drown them out. Bird identification became our hobby while we traced the canal, marveling at the stillness of the human world and the busyness of everything else.

It was while taking a slightly modified route that we noticed the missing cat signs. At first it was just the one: Dumpy was a ginger that lived a block above us. No reward, just a black and white picture showing his narrow face and pert little ears looking up at us with an endearing curiosity.

We laughed at the name and carried on. Then we started noticing other lost cat signs festooning the telephone poles all around our area.

We have moved to Ottawa in January. Though I'd agreed to it, I don't like Ottawa. It's too spread out and there's a dead-end feeling to the place. I missed Montreal before we even moved, saying goodbye to Verdun and visiting all my favourite bars and coffee shops before we left.

"It's not like it's that far," Colin would say.

I agreed to move because I love Colin and he was offered a great job. I picked up a teaching gig for the winter semester and bowed my head to the whole thing, telling myself that I would write in the evenings.

All this to say we were relatively new to the neighbourhood when the pandemic hit and when we started seeing the lost cat posters. Once upon a time we'd contemplated getting a cat before quickly discovering we were both allergic. Still, we agreed we were cat people, if only in spirit.

Dumpy was followed by a tabby named Martin, then Holly and then Murph, a white fluffy number, whose owner was offering five hundred dollars for his safe return.

"This is getting weird, right?" I said during one of our walks, as we made our way past the curling arena towards

Dundonald park.

"I don't know, is it?"

"Well when have you ever seen this many lost cat posters?"

"Maybe I've just never noticed them before. Let's go this way," said Colin.

We turned on to McLaren, a street filled with old houses turned into apartments, with the exception of one or two new condos.

"Think we'll ever be able to afford these places?"

"Not unless you write the next Harry Potter."

Our walks normally coincided with the outdoor activities of our neighbours on the block. There was a group of them that seemed to all know each other and had kids the same age. If it was nice and not too cold, they'd often congregate on the sidewalks at lunchtime, chatting while the kids drew on the pavement with chalk.

They did not talk to us. In fact, if they acknowledged us at all, it was with a frown, or a blank stare, even if I was giving them my most gracious, kid-loving smile.

"You ever notice that the neighbours look at us like we're going to kidnap their kids?" said Colin one sunny afternoon.

"I mean, we're keeping our distance, what's their problem?"

I was as clueless as he was. The weird thing was, as the number of missing cats grew, so too did the hostility of our neighbours.

My class finished at the beginning of April. I was bored. Colin was busy as ever, working odd hours now because of talks with a client in Taiwan. He'd get up at six in the morning, have a nap at noon and then work again until midnight.

I started going on long walks alone. There was still the occasional flurry blowing down the streets. This only made a walk more appealing, after being cooped up in our apartment for so long. I felt a connection with the other walkers, who I decided were also bored, restless, childless and jobless. They were mostly young, though some were much older. I steered clear of obviously elderly. Everyone did. Didn't want to give them COVID, after all.

My walks got longer, until I was spending most of my afternoons outdoors, crossing the Corktown bridge into Sandy Hill, marveling at how quiet the Ottawa University campus was. I walked through Strathcona Park and along the river, coming back through Lowertown before taking a breather at the National Art Gallery. I started packing snacks and water in a backpack.

I grew up in Ottawa. I know the city well. There isn't much that could surprise me about the place. Missing cat posters plastering telephone poles all over downtown made it feel sinister. Suddenly it was a city with dark secrets, exposed by the lockdown. I saw at least one or two new posters on every one of my walks. Initially I just thought the original cat owners had widened their search range. But when I really started paying attention, I realized there were more cats missing. Twenty in all.

"Can you believe it?" I said to Colin, pausing the show we were watching over dinner one night.

"It's pretty crazy."

"Do you think they might all be connected? It just seems so weird that all those cats would vanish at the same time."

"No idea."

"Do you think our neighbours hate us because they think we're cat murderers?"

Not even a chuckle. I rolled my eyes. When Colin was focused on something, everything else was irritating background noise. He finished eating before the show ended and went back to his office.

"I'm sorry," he said when he came to bed. "Look if you find anything weird out, let me know okay?"

"It'd be more fun if you came with me sometimes."

Colin shook his head.

"This is a really important account."

He kissed me and rolled over. I decided to go out again to take pictures of all the cat posters I could find.

THE NEXT DAY I PRINTED OFF A MAP OF THE CITY AND started putting red dots where I'd found each poster. Some posters had names on them, or email addresses or even home addresses. All helpful information for cat rescuers or burglars.

I had postal codes for twelve of the twenty cats. All twelve were missing from within a kilometer radius. A tiny area for so many cats to go missing from.

There was no discernible pattern, in terms of size, sex or colour. The cats ranged from tabby to calico to purebred, though I wondered why on Earth someone would let a two-thousand-dollar cat just wander around the streets at night.

I started re-orienting my walk routes. If I noticed a cluster of people, all respectfully distanced in heated discussion, I would walk towards them, mask on, headphones in so they'd think I wasn't listening.

Most, admittedly, were talking about the coronavirus. Hard to blame them. But occasionally there were useful snippets.

"Have you heard from Angie lately?"

"No poor thing is still so upset about Mitsy."

"We should bring her some food or something, so hard when you're all alone like that..."

What I really wanted to do was ask some questions, except the neighbours remained a separate mystery to me. Standoffish even when they're own kids would run up and say hi. It would be a dead end, I knew. I smiled as usual and continued walking past.

FRIDAY NIGHT, I TOLD COLIN HE HAD TO COME OUT WITH me.

"It'll be our date night."

"We see each other literally all the time."

"Yeah, but we barely talk! I want to talk with you, let's have a chat, let's catch up." Colin smirked.

"You know what I've been doing all week."

"Oh god Colin come on please, just for a short walk."

We walked south through the Glebe. It was brisk despite the buds on the trees. A new house was being built. We argued about whether it was a single home or condos.

"Condos doesn't fit the style of the place," said Colin

"There are condo buildings everywhere. They're just not the ugly towers that's all."

"This one's boutique."

"Exactly," I laughed. "Luxury in a slightly larger box with fewer neighbours."

"I still think it's one guy's house."

"Who has that kind of money here?"

We walked back down Percy under the highway when I saw him. Dumpy. He was ginger, just like the poster described, with a speck of white at the tip of his tail. He was on the corner of Catherine under lamplight, looking right at us.

"Oh my god," I said, grabbing Colin's arm and pointing.

"What?"

"Look! It's Dumpy!"

"Who?"

Ignoring him, I let go and walked cautiously towards Dumpy. His butt was facing me now, so I couldn't get a good look at its face, couldn't see if he had the little flecks of white that looked like dimples next to his little pink nose. I skipped across Catherine, and in response Colin yelled out. He hates when I jaywalk. I shushed him, waving a hand behind me and continued to pursue Dumpy. He was walking towards Percy, about to turn left.

Dumpy seemed entirely unconcerned about being followed. I jogged closer until I was right behind him.

"Hey buddy, where've you—"

"What are you doing?"

I looked up. A woman was standing on her front porch, staring at me in alarm.

"I thought this was one of the missing cats. From the posters."

The woman rushed over and picked up the cat.

"This is my cat Cali."

"I'm so sorry I thought it was one of the missing ones, have you seen those posters for a missing cat called Dumpy?"

"Excuse me?"

"He, there were pictures posted around here, he looks a lot like yours."

At this point Colin had caught up to us and put his hand on my shoulder.

"Sorry, uh, ma'am, my girlfriend is really obsessed with these lost cats."

"Obsessed is a bit strong."

Colin was steering me away while the woman watched us, Cali protectively nestled in her arms.

"Don't touch my cat!" she said, then slammed the door.

"Jesus, why did you say that?" I said to Colin as we made our way back to the apartment.

"You were not winning with that woman. Better to just walk away."

"Okay but did you have to say that thing about being obsessed?"

"Hey, look it just slipped out. I didn't mean anything by it."

"Yeah, sure."

"What's that supposed to mean?"

"I don't have colleagues to talk to everyday Colin, and we can't see any of our friends, or our parents, so what exactly do you expect me to do with my time? How would you like to see it better spent?"

He sighed. "Do what you want. I said it didn't mean anything."

"Well I'm saying I don't believe you."

He said nothing. Unlocked the door.

"Why don't you just tell me what your problem is? Is it because I'm not writing enough? You think I'm being lazy?"

"Okay that's enough. You're reading way too much into one stupid sentence. I said it didn't mean anything, can we just drop it? You are clearly the one feeling guilty or something for spending all your time thinking about these cats."

I didn't respond. Instead I went to the kitchen and

searched in the cupboard for some chocolate.

"Goddammit did you finish off the last chocolate bar?" I yelled.

"I'm going for a drive," said Colin.

I waited for an hour to see if he would come home, so I could apologize. He didn't come home. Maybe he'd gone to his brother's place to have a beer and blow off some steam. Breaking lockdown rules, but I wasn't going to bring that up.

Around nine, with still no sign of Colin I decided to go for another walk, half-expecting to see the words "Cat Killer" scrawled on our building's front door. The corner store was still open, so I went in and grabbed an ice cream bar. A poor supplement for the comfort of chocolate I was craving.

I replicated our earlier walk. Past the construction site until I hit a towering church off Fourth. Near one of the side doors was a message board. No lost cat posters here.

Something was rubbing on my leg. I looked down and there was Dumpy. The real Dumpy this time, I was sure of it. I knelt down to rub his head and he proceeded to lay on his back and mewl. There was the white speck on his tail, there were the two dimples. I wasn't making a mistake this time.

Then I heard a tinkling sound and looked down the street. There were lights on at a house a few paces down, and a woman waving a bell. Dumpy seemed to recognize the sound because he flipped off his back and meandered towards it. I stood there watching him and saw at least two other cats drift into the porch light. I walked towards the house, careful to appear casual. I'm taking a walk, I said to myself. I'm taking a walk and its perfectly natural to slow down a bit when I see fifteen cats on some lady's porch slurping milk

117

from saucers.

I recognized all but two of them. Some were still wearing their collars. The woman, dressed in boots and a winter jacket, was crouched down next to them, stroking their heads and murmuring.

"Wow," I said.

The woman stood up fast enough that a few cats pulled their heads back abruptly from their milk.

"Oh my goodness. You scared me."

Her house was huge. The woman, in comparison, was short and a little hunched over. Her hair was tied in a loose bun, strands gently falling behind her ears.

"That's a lot of cats," I said, figuring I might as well get straight to the point.

The woman looked down.

"Yes. I suppose it is." She looked at me. "It's been nice to have a bit of company, with everything going on."

"Are...are they all yours?"

"Well," said the woman smiling. "I don't know if I'd call them my cats, they do as they please. All I know is they always come when I tinkle the little bell. They do enjoy the milk."

"Definitely seems to be the case."

"They've all got their own personalities I'm noticing. Haven't given them all names yet, waiting to see what fits best."

"Do you live alone?" I asked, coming a bit closer to the porch steps.

She nodded. "My husband died last year."

"I'm sorry."

"If I'd known we'd be living through a pandemic I might've planned to move to the country."

She focused on me now that I was in the porchlight.

"At least I wasn't in Florida like a few people I know."

"Or on a cruise." She laughed in agreement.

"Do you let them all inside?" I gestured at the now satiated cats.

"When it's cold, yes. Don't seem to have any other place to go."

"It's nice that you take care of them."

"Nice to have something to do. They're the only friends I get to see these days."

I smiled in what I hoped was an understanding way.

"I'd better head off," I said. "Have a good evening."

"You too," she said, shuttling cats into her front door.

I walked to the end of the street, then waited until she'd gone in and the light was off. Then I went back and noted the address.

When I came home, Colin was back. He hugged me.

"It was stupid what I said to that woman."

"I said some stupid things too. We're even."

He hugged me tighter.

"I know I need to prioritize our time together more. I'll try to be better."

"I know you don't care what I do with my time. It's just, writing, teaching, it all seems so pointless now, you know? I guess I wanted to do something concrete. Help people."

"I get that."

I told him about my evening adventure, and he asked me what I was going to do. I didn't know.

I CALLED ALL THE NUMBERS ON THE MISSING CAT POSTERS and gave them the woman's address. I told them she was

119

taking care of a large number of cats, maybe she thought they were strays, and that she must not have seen any of the posters. I said all the cats looked perfectly healthy. One woman burst into tears.

"Oh my god I thought he was dead," she cried over the phone.

I let a month pass before going back to the woman's place. When I finally went by, there was a for sale sign on the lawn and the place looked empty. The worst-case scenario crossed my mind. Or it could be she was downsizing. Things were slowly opening up, and even in a pandemic there'd surely be buyers for a place like this. I looked around, pleased to see a crab apple tree in bloom. We'd just had our first in-person visit with a friend on our front lawn and I felt lighter than I had in a while. A cat a few houses down was stalking a pigeon on the sidewalk. It looked pretty tubby. Not one I recognized. The pigeon flew off. The cat came over and pushed up against my legs. I rubbed its head, hoping it had a home. Then I continued my walk.

About the Author

Emma Bider is a writer, editor and perpetual student. Her fiction has been published in two anthologies, *Voices Rise* and *The Shepherd*. Her poetry has been published on *The Unpublishable Zine* website, and in the poetry anthology *The Dark Room*. We Animals is her first short story collection. Follow Emma on Twitter @ebider, or say hello and leave a review on her website, emmarbider.com. She will respond, and possibly start a conversation with you about books. Emma lives in Ottawa and is currently trying to identify all the trees in her neighbourhood.

THANKS FOR READING!

PLEASE ADD A SHORT REVIEW ON AMAZON

AND LET ME KNOW WHAT YOU THOUGHT!